CONTENTS

Foreword — vii

Introduction — ix

STEP ONE: Sleep — 1

STEP TWO: Hydrate — 16

STEP THREE: Nourish — 27

STEP FOUR: Move — 51

STEP FIVE: Digest — 64

STEP SIX: Alkalise — 75

STEP SEVEN: Breathe — 85

STEP EIGHT: Supplement — 97

STEP NINE: Love — 105

STEP TEN: Prevent — 121

STEP ELEVEN: Moderate — 133

STEP TWELVE: Relax — 156

STEP THIRTEEN: Rejoice — 167

STEP FOURTEEN: Personalise — 185

References — 195

FOREWORD

When I had just finished writing *13 Steps to Bloody Good Wealth* along with Sunil Dalal, I received an email that said 'Ashwin, please remember that health is more important than wealth.' That email was from Dr Mukesh Batra. It resulted in a phone conversation that same day and an interesting lunch a week later.

Over a khichdi meal, I told Dr Batra that readers would laugh at me if I wrote a book about health because one simply needs to look at me to realise that everything about me is the exact opposite—my weight, my drinking, my cigar smoking ... the list is endless. I am probably one of the unhealthiest people on the planet!

Dr Batra smiled and reminded me of a line from Tolstoy: Everyone thinks of changing the world, but no one thinks of changing himself. He looked at me and said, 'Why don't you look at this book as a journey? Along the way, you may pick up a few tips that may make you healthier.' I reluctantly agreed to go along, but my overall views were still rather fixed. I almost believed in the maxim that living healthy was merely the slowest possible rate at which you could die.

And then the book outline emerged and each chapter began taking shape. And before I knew what was happening, I found myself attempting to implement some of the suggestions. In the eighteen months that we worked on this book, I lost some weight, began sleeping better and was able to cut out foolish medications that I had been consuming out of mere habit. My bad habits remained but I was now more aware of them. In fact, I found myself regularly reminded of Leon Eldred's words: 'If I'd known I was going to live so long, I'd have taken better care of myself.'

The unfortunate truth is that inside every older person is a younger person wondering what in the world went wrong. And life's tragedy is that we get old too soon and wise too late. There are so many things that I could have done and so many things I should have done to be healthier. And that's precisely the reason why this book was needed—to compensate for the error of my ways.

That's also the reason why this book had to be written by Dr Batra. As you know, most books in the *13 Steps* series are driven by the vertical domain knowledge of my co-authors and the expertise of Dr Batra shines through in this book. I couldn't really imagine any better partner to write this book with. He is absolutely brilliant.

There is an old Chinese proverb that says, 'It is easy to get a thousand prescriptions but hard to get one single remedy.' Dr Batra disproves that proverb with this book which focuses on simple things that even utterly unhealthy folks like me can implement.

Ashwin Sanghi
Mumbai, 2018

13 STEPS TO BLOODY GOOD HEALTH

Ashwin Sanghi is counted among India's highest selling English authors. He has written several bestsellers (*The Rozabal Line, Chanakya's Chant, The Krishna Key, The Sialkot Saga, Keepers of the Kalachakra, The Vault of Vishnu,* and *The Magicians of Mazda* in his *Bharat Series*) and two *New York Times* bestselling crime thrillers with James Patterson, *Private India* (sold in the US as *City on Fire*) and *Private Delhi* (sold in the US as *Count to Ten*). Ashwin also mentors, co-writes and edits titles in this popular *13 Steps Series* on subjects as diverse as Luck, Wealth, Marks, Health and Parenting.

He is a regular contributor to the Op-Ed pages of the *Times of India*. Ashwin has been included by *Forbes India* in their Celebrity 100 and by the *New Indian Express* in their Culture Power List. He is a winner of the Crossword Popular Choice Award 2012, Atta Galatta Popular Choice Award 2018, WBR Iconic Achievers Award 2018, the Lit-O-Fest Literature Legend Award 2018, the Kalinga Popular Choice Award 2021 and the Deendayal Upadhyaya Recognition 2023. He was educated at Cathedral and John Connon School, Mumbai, and St Xavier's College, Mumbai. He holds a Master's from Yale University, USA, and a D. Litt. (Honoris Causa) from JECRC University, Rajasthan. Ashwin lives in Mumbai with his wife, Anushika, and his son, Raghuvir.

Website: www.sanghi.in
Facebook: www.facebook.com/ashwinsanghi
Twitter: www.twitter.com/ashwinsanghi
YouTube: www.youtube.com/ashwinsanghi
Instagram: instagram.com/ashwin.sanghi
LinkedIn: www.linkedin.com/in/ashwinsanghi

Dr Mukesh Batra, homeopath of international repute, is the founder-chairman of Dr Batra's™ Group, the world's first and largest homeopathy corporate. In a career spanning four decades, Dr Batra has treated over a million patients, including eminent political leaders, presidents and prime ministers, prominent film personalities and industrialists. He has been honoured with several fellowships and over fifty national and international awards, including the Padma Shri, one of India's highest civilian honours by the President of India. Dr Batra is the first Asian homeopath to be awarded honorary fellowships by both the British and American homeopathic associations. A film based on his work is course material for post graduate students of homeopathy worldwide. He has published several research papers in national and international professional and scientific journals. Dr Batra has popularised homeopathy through his writing in newspapers, magazines and books. His book, *Everyman's Guide to Homeopathy*, was a national bestseller and has been published in multiple languages in three editions. His other book, *Healing with Homeopathy* is already in its third edition. He also extends homeopathic care to animal welfare shelters, orphanges and old-age homes. His own personal interests include photography and singing, and have been turned into exhibitions and concerts that raise funds for charitable causes.

You can connect with Dr Batra via the following channels:

Website: www.drbatras.com
Facebook: www.facebook.com/DrBatrasHealthcare/
Youtube: www.youtube.com/user/Drbatrasgroup
Instagram: www.instagram.com/dr.mukeshbatra/

13 STEPS TO BLOODY GOOD HEALTH

**ASHWIN SANGHI
DR MUKESH BATRA**

First published by Westland Publications Private Limited in 2018

Published by Westland Books, a division of Nasadiya Technologies Private Limited in 2023

No. 269/2B, First Floor, 'Irai Arul', Vimalraj Street, Nethaji Nagar, Alapakkam Main Road, Maduravoyal, Chennai 600095

Westland and the Westland logo are the trademarks of Nasadiya Technologies Private Limited, or its affiliates.

Copyright © Ashwin Sanghi, 2018

Ashwin Sanghi asserts the moral right to be identified as the author of this work.

ISBN: ISBN: 9789395767798

10 9 8 7 6 5 4 3 2 1

The views and opinions expressed in this work are the author's own and the facts are as reported by him, and the publisher is in no way liable for the same.

All rights reserved

Typeset in Arno Pro by SÜRYA, New Delhi
Printed at Nutech Print Services-India

No part of this book may be reproduced, or stored in a retrieval system, or transmitted in any form or by any means, electronic, mechanical, photocopying, recording, or otherwise, without express written permission of the publisher.

INTRODUCTION

In over forty-four years of my medical practice, I have realised that the key to a happy and healthy life is often simple. The secret foods for good health are in our kitchens while we keep searching for them on the Internet.

We spend money on 'health fads', which are often unnecessary and sometimes even dangerous. I therefore thought if I could pen down the thirteen most important things for good health that often get overlooked, it could motivate people to live happier and healthier lives.

Having known that Ashwin was writing the *13 Steps* series, I felt that good health was missing from his life and writings. If by writing this book, he could pick up a few health tips, we would have a healthier ace writer around for a longer time. As Ashley Montagu said, 'The idea is to die young as late as possible!'

Ashwin is not only a great writer, but also a fabulous storyteller and his writing and communication skills could be used to convey strong messages of good health in simple and easy-to-implement ways. Ashwin often jokes that he writes fiction, makes up stories, and thus everything he writes could be considered a lie. I thought that I could get him to narrate some truths in an enjoyable way.

It is often the simplest things that we overlook in our pursuit of wealth and happiness. However, without good health there is no wealth or happiness. People who do not prioritise their health, inevitably end up having to prioritise their sickness. I hope that through this book, readers will pick up small, easy-to-do common sense tips to achieve good health and live happier and healthier lives.

Mukesh Batra
Mumbai, 2018

STEP ONE: SLEEP

The British writer Edward Lucas rightly observed, 'There is more refreshment and stimulation in a nap, even of the briefest, than in all the alcohol ever distilled.' Rings true, right? Unfortunately, most of us do not realise the importance of sleep for our health and well-being. 'Having peace, happiness, and healthiness is my definition of beauty and you can't have any of that without sleep,' says the American singer and songwriter Beyoncé.

More important than food or water

So how important is sleep in comparison to food or water for the human body? Well, under normal conditions, a human being (depending on size, activity level and the amount of fat stored in the body) can live for more than three weeks without food. In exceptional cases, one can live even longer. Mahatma Gandhi survived twenty-one days of complete starvation whereas, according to some records, Bhagat Singh and his followers went on a hunger strike for 116 days! Without water, one can survive for about a week in normal conditions. But when you go without sleep even for twenty to twenty-five hours, your performance impairment becomes equivalent to that of someone who has a blood alcohol level of 0.10 per cent. At thirty-six, forty-eight, and seventy-two hours without sleep, your body and mind begin operating in altered states that can even result in death. Effectively, your body can actually go a little longer without food and water than it does without sleep!

India is sleep-deprived

The actress Gwyneth Paltrow says, 'For me, sleep is a major thing. I don't always get it and when I don't, I look like I have been hit by a truck.' Consistently getting seven to eight hours of sleep every night is important for good health. Any less not only affects your mood and energy levels the next day, but can also increase your risk for serious chronic health conditions. But are we getting sufficient sleep today? Statistics convey an unsettling story. According to an Indian sleep survey conducted by a leading consumer products brand:

- About 93 per cent of Indians are sleep-deprived.
- Around 72 per cent of Indians wake up one to three times per night.
- Around 87 per cent of the Indian population confirms that lack of sleep is affecting their health.
- More than 58 per cent of Indians believe their work suffers due to lack of adequate sleep.
- About 38 per cent have witnessed a colleague falling asleep at work.

What do these figures suggest? The situation is summed up by Arianna Huffington, the co-founder of *The Huffington Post*: 'We are in the midst of a sleep deprivation crisis. And this has profound consequences—on our health, our job performance, our relationships and our happiness. What is needed is nothing short of a sleep revolution. Only by renewing our relationship with sleep can we take back control of our lives.'

What causes poor sleep?

So why are people spending sleepless nights? Unfortunately, many factors interfere with natural sleep patterns. Some of the factors that can affect your sleep are:

- Pain such as body aches, headaches, toothaches
- Itching associated with psoriasis, eczema, and other skin conditions
- Medical disorders such as nose blocks, asthma, breathlessness and coughing
- Psychiatric disorders like depression and anxiety
- Addictions such as alcohol, caffeine, drug abuse or digital addiction
- Stress, for example, due to job loss, death of a loved one, divorce or moving homes
- Acidity causing ulcers, heartburn or acid reflux
- Irritable bowels thus causing frequent trips to the bathroom
- Environmental factors such as light, noise, or extreme temperatures

- Lifestyle patterns such as working night shifts, extensive business travel, emergency medical duty and so on

Quantity versus quality

Not only the quantity of sleep but also the quality of sleep has declined over the years. According to the National Sleep Foundation, the key indicators of good sleep quality, as established by a panel of experts, are as follows:

- Sleeping for more time while in bed (at least 85 per cent of the total time)
- Falling asleep in thirty minutes or less
- Waking up no more than once per night
- Being awake for a break of less than twenty minutes during sleeping hours

It is a fallacy to think of sleep as merely a state of inactivity. Broadly, there are two stages of sleep—Non-Rapid Eye Movement (NREM) Sleep and Rapid Eye Movement (REM) Sleep.

- NREM sleep is the type of sleep when you don't dream. It is what most people associate with sleep. It is a very relaxed type of sleep that gets progressively deeper (with your brainwaves getting progressively slower) through three stages called N1, N2 and N3.
- REM sleep is your dream state. Your eyes move rapidly. It's a rather active sort of sleep in which the brain is almost as active as if it were awake. REM sleep is also called paradoxical sleep because you only look like

you're fast asleep but there's a ton of stuff happening inside your brain.

The body cycles between NREM and REM every ninety minutes. This is known as the sleep cycle. For most people, the first REM period may be just five minutes, the second, ten minutes, and the third, fifteen minutes. Your last dream of the night can last for thirty to sixty minutes. Remember, you may or may not recall dreaming, but *everyone* dreams each night.

Having a complete sleep cycle is important because each type of sleep has its own specific benefits. For example, some of the things happening to you when you are in deep NREM (N3) are:

- Wounds get healed
- Your energy is restored and your body undergoes maintenance
- White blood cells are created to prop up your body's defense mechanism
- Your muscles are relaxed and restored
- Growth hormones are released
- The brain reorganises the mental pathways within the cortex, an activity vital to learning and to brain development

Thus, NREM is probably the most important part of your sleep. When you are deprived of NREM, your body tries to make up for it whenever it can.

The big question: why have REM sleep at all? Why doesn't the body simply slip into NREM-N3 and stay there? Why have cyclical REM interruptions at all? Well, the answer is rather simple. If you're awake, the significant mental stimulus to the brain comes from your surroundings, but when you're in REM, all your mental stimulus is created by the brain itself. It is this internal stimulus that assists in processing memories and building new skills.

During REM, your brain is buzzing but your body isn't and so this is the ideal time for the brain to reorganise and refile thoughts, skills and memories of the day. Dreams, which account for a significant part of REM sleep, are also believed to help in this process. Research has shown that songbirds practice new mating calls in their dreams—calls that they had originally heard when awake.

Need for sleep varies across individuals

Most people take sleep for granted. But remember that sleep affects you more than you think. When you sleep, your body heals itself every day. That is why you should get the required hours of sleep every day. You can't sleep less during week days and try to make up for it by sleeping more than required on weekends.

The famous singer, Jennifer Lopez, has been known to say that 'Sleep is my weapon. I try to get eight hours of sleep. I think what works best is sleep, water… and a good cleanser!'

The American satirist Bill Hicks quipped, 'I'm so tired. I need my sleep. I make no bones about it. I need eight hours a day. And at least ten at night.'

Where do you figure on the spectrum of sleeping hours?

Well, every individual's need for sleep varies. In general, most healthy adults need an average of eight hours of sleep every night. However, some individuals are able to function without sleepiness or drowsiness after as little as six hours of sleep. Others can't perform at their peak unless they've slept ten hours. And, contrary to the common myth, the need for sleep doesn't decline with age. Rather, according to the *Principles & Practice of Sleep Medicine*, by Van Dongen and Dinges, it is the *ability* to sleep for six to eight hours at a given time rather than the *need* that probably reduces with age.

Critical for children

Sleep is even more important for the well-being of children, as it directly impacts their mental and physical development. During the deep state of sleep, blood supply to the muscles is increased, energy is restored, tissue repair occurs and important hormones are released for growth and development. Consider the number of hours of sleep that children require:

- For toddlers (1 - 2 years) – 11 to 14 hours per day
- Preschoolers (3 - 5 years) – 10 to 13 hours per day
- Older children (6 - 13 years) – 9 to 11 hours per day
- Teenagers (14 - 17 years) – 8 to 10 hours per day

Inability to fight infection or disease

Sleep deprivation prevents our immune system from marshalling forces to fight the foreign bodies that cause infections. This means that our bodies may be unable to fend off invaders. For example, sleep is involved in healing and the repair of our heart and blood vessels and ongoing sleep deficiency is linked to an increased risk of heart disease, kidney disease, high blood pressure, diabetes and stroke.

Sleep deprivation can also be a cause of weight gain

Singer Christina Aguilera has quipped, 'People spend money on beauty potions, but a good night's rest makes all the difference.' There is much truth in her quip. People who sleep less tend to weigh significantly more than those who get adequate sleep.

Consider the case of Aditi, a seventeen-year-old girl who visited our clinic for obesity. She specifically mentioned that she did not overeat and that she even exercised moderately. However, she had been putting on a lot of weight. No diet or exercise regimen seemed to be helping. After a detailed analysis of her diet, work, exercise and sleep patterns, we discovered that Aditi had sleep issues. She was rarely sleeping for more than four hours per day. We estimated this to be the reason for her sudden weight gain. She was advised to sleep at least for eight to nine hours daily. We also suggested an appropriate diet and exercise regimen. As a cumulative effect, Aditi started losing weight slowly but steadily. It was magical, she said. She had never thought that sleep could affect her health so much.

Why is your weight related to your sleep? The effect of sleep on weight gain is believed to be caused by numerous factors, including hormones and motivation to exercise.

Good sleepers tend to eat less calories, whereas sleep-deprived individuals have a bigger appetite and tend to eat more. Sleep deprivation disrupts the daily fluctuations in appetite hormones and is believed to cause poor appetite regulation. This includes high levels of ghrelin, the hormone that stimulates appetite, and reduced levels of leptin, the hormone that suppresses appetite. So if you are trying to lose weight, make sure you are getting sufficient sleep.

Important for brain function

Actress Halle Berry says, 'I love to sleep. When I am rested, I'm at my best.' Sleep is important for various aspects of brain function. This includes cognition, concentration, productivity and performance. All of these are negatively affected by sleep deprivation. A study performed on medical interns proves this. Interns who did not have enough sleep made 36 per cent more serious medical errors than interns who slept properly. Sleep deprivation can negatively impact some aspects of brain function to as great a degree as intoxication. Good sleep, on the other hand, improves problem-solving skills and enhances memory performance in both children and adults. Consider the following example:

Mohit is a thirty-two-year-old medical representative. His job is to increase product awareness, answer queries, provide advice and introduce new products to doctors and other medical professionals. He was a bright student back in college but of late was finding it extremely difficult to focus on his work, particularly when it came to memorising or presenting certain details about his products. It was getting increasingly difficult for Mohit to meet his targets. It affected him professionally and this gradually led to depression. He tried anti-depressants but they worked only temporarily. He finally decided to take medical help and was diagnosed with sleep deficiency. Mohit was sleeping for only three to four hours at night. This was the reason behind his poor memory, reduced concentration and reduced work efficiency. Treatment focus was shifted to improving his sleep quality and the results were amazing. He now has an improved memory and his concentration levels have improved, too.

Sleep can also maximise athletic performance

The modern athlete knows that physical conditioning and good nutrition are critical in reaching peak athletic performance; however, sleep, while often overlooked, plays an equally important role.

In fact, the quality and quantity of sleep obtained can be the edge between winning and losing on a game day. If you tell an athlete that there is a treatment that would reduce the chemicals associated with stress, naturally increase human growth hormone and also enhance recovery rate along with improving performance, they would all rush to take that treatment. Sleep does it all.

In a study on basketball players, longer sleep was shown to significantly improve speed, accuracy, reaction times and mental well-being. On the other hand, a study of over 2,800 women found that poor sleep was linked to slower walking, lower grip strength and greater difficulty performing independent activities. Beyond acute injuries, one recent study on Major League baseball players has shown fatigue can shorten the playing careers of professional athletes.

Sleep disorders are one of the major causes of accidents

According to the National Highway Safety Administration, falling asleep while driving is responsible for at least 100,000 crashes, 71,000 injuries and 1,550 deaths each year in the United States. It is estimated that nearly 20 per cent of all accidents are caused by fatigue as per the UK's Royal Society for Prevention of Accidents.

Sleep deprivation is linked to substance abuse

According to a long-term study published in the 2004 April issue of *Alcoholism: Clinical and Experimental Research*, young teenagers whose preschool sleep habits were poor were more than twice as likely to use drugs, tobacco or alcohol.

Poor sleep is linked to depression

It has been estimated that 90 per cent of patients with depression complain about sleep quality. Poor sleep is even associated with increased risk of death by suicide. Those with sleeping disorders, such as insomnia or obstructive sleep apnea, also report significantly higher rates of depression than those without.

Good sleep can enhance your performance at work

Good sleep affects you more than you think. Here are the key benefits that meeting your sleep quota can ensure:

- Enhancing decision-making skills
- Improving memory and concentration
- Increasing work efficiency
- Widening attention span
- Increasing alertness

What can you do to sleep better?

The National Sleep Foundation has a few tips for sleeping better. Most of them are rather easy to implement.

- Block out light: All humans have a natural built-in clock known as the circadian rhythm. It sends signals to our bodies when it is day or night so that you may wake or sleep. In the evening, when it's dark, your circadian rhythm triggers the release of melatonin—a hormone that makes you sleepy. Light in your bedroom interferes with that process. Turn off the lights, avoid keeping the television turned on, use blackout curtains or an eye mask to sleep better.
- Avoid handheld devices: Light from handheld devices can interfere with melatonin production. If you must use such devices, switch them to night mode.
- Read: Kids love hearing bedtime stories before they sleep. When we grow up, we forget that we, too, were kids once. Reading can help clear your mind of your worries and troubles and lull you into a comfortable mental space.

- Avoid afternoon naps: I can't seem to recall who joked, 'I've reached that age when happy hour is a nap.' Daytime naps—what are often called power naps—are mentioned these days as productivity boosters. Unfortunately, they can be counter-productive as they tend to disrupt your nightly sleep pattern. If you find that a nap is imperative, use a nap tracker app to ensure that you do not oversleep. Twenty minutes is the ideal duration because you are prevented from entering deep sleep.
- Melatonin supplements: A melatonin supplement can be an option to fall asleep faster and improve sleep quality. In some countries, you may require a doctor's prescription for a melatonin supplement. There are other options such as ginkgo biloba, glycin, valerian root, magnesium, L-theanine and lavender. Please take appropriate medical advice before starting any natural supplement. The one supplement that you do not need to take advice for is a time-tested grandmothers' remedy—warm milk. It's a natural melatonin booster owing to its calcium content.
- Follow a routine: Set a bedtime and wake-up time and follow it, even on weekends. Sticking to a schedule regulates your body clock and you will eventually find yourself feeling sleepy at your usual bedtime.
- Exercise regularly: Exercise seems to help improve sleep quality. According to a recent study, just 150 minutes of moderate to vigorous exercise per week can ensure that you fall asleep on time. Moreover, it can ensure that your sleep quality is improved. Remember though

that exercise time must not eat into sleeping time. Furthermore, avoid exercising late in the day.
- Manage your bedroom temperature and noise: Experts say that a room temperature of 18 degrees Celsius is ideal for sleep but you can judge what temperature setting works best for you. The golden rule is that you should not feel either too hot or too cold at any time during the night. Your bedroom should be free from noises that can disrupt your sleep. This could include a partner's sounds such as snoring. Use ear plugs or white noise machines in such cases.
- Avoid alcohol and heavy meals in the evening: Eating a heavy meal or consuming alcohol at night can cause indigestion, flatulence or acidity. Any of these side-effects would interfere with falling asleep. Keep evening meals light and try to eat a couple of hours before bedtime.
- Practice a relaxing bedtime ritual: For example, a meditative routine or prayer can help. There are many apps that can help you with soothing sounds or guided meditation routines. A hot bath or shower before sleeping is another option.
- Avoid stimulants and too many liquids at night: Caffeine, nicotine and other stimulants should be avoided.
- Limit fluid intake: Nocturia is the medical term for excessive urination during the night. You can avoid nocturia by limiting your fluid intake before sleep.
- Sleep on a comfortable mattress and pillows: Your mattress and pillows should be comfortable and supportive. Check that they haven't become too old. Ensure that they are free of allergens.

Key Takeaways

- Sleep is more important than food or water.
- Poor sleep can be caused by a multitude of factors including pain, stress, acidity, irritable bowels, depression, environment, etc.
- Getting adequate quantity and quality of both REM and NREM sleep is vital.
- During the sleep cycle, your body undergoes maintenance; growth hormones are released and wounds are healed. It also helps in processing memories and building new skills.
- Lack of sleep can cause poor immunity, obesity, depression and even substance abuse. Good sleep can enhance athletic performance, memory, decision-making and brain function.
- You can sleep better by blocking out noise and light, taking melatonin supplements, following a routine, exercising regularly, managing room temperature, avoiding heavy meals and alcohol or stimulants before bedtime, limiting fluid intake and sleeping on a comfortable mattress and pillows.

STEP TWO: HYDRATE

'I never drink water; that's the stuff that rusts pipes,' said W.C. Fields, the American comedian. I wonder what his insides looked like! Jokes apart, the truth is that water is the elixir of life. Read on to find out why.

Your body is a reflection of the earth

Three-fourths of the earth's surface is covered by water. The human body should actually mirror that. At birth, water makes up 80 per cent of your body weight. As an adult, you should be 70 per cent water.

The necessity of rehydration

Alice Roosevelt Longworth wittily observed, 'Fill what's empty, empty what's full, and scratch where it itches.' Every cell in our body needs water to keep functioning. Our body uses water in all its organs, and tissues to help regulate its temperature and carry out its vital functions. Because it loses water through breathing, sweating and digestion, it's important to rehydrate by drinking fluids and eating foods that contain water.

Fine, so we know that water is important for survival. Unfortunately, we still do not drink enough of it. How often do you feel the sensation of thirst on a daily basis? You may actually feel it as you read this chapter. That sensation is actually your body sending a signal to your brain that it is getting dehydrated.

But remember:

- Do not have a lot of water at one go if you suffer from dehydration headache.
- Drink small amounts frequently—say 200-250 ml every hour.
- Electrolytes play an essential role in water retention. Failure to replace lost electrolytes will lead to difficulties in rehydrating. Add some electrolyte powder to your water for fast electrolyte replenishment.

Also remember that some foods have high water content. Including them in your diet can also hydrate your body. Examples are watermelon (almost entirely water, 92 per cent to be precise), strawberries (equally high water content), cantaloupe, pineapple, oranges, raspberries, iceberg lettuce, celery and spinach.

Signs of dehydration

How would you know that you are dehydrated? For this, you need to know some of the symptoms of dehydration. Some common symptoms are:

- Dry mouth
- Drowsiness

- Thirst
- Headaches
- Constipation
- Dizziness

Water when consumed the right way will not only quench your thirst but also do a lot of good to your body. It is one of the best medicines you can take to keep your body running fine.

Why should you drink water? There are abundant reasons. Let's examine some of them:

- Water helps your body detox: A simple day-to-day routine is to have a full glass of water first thing in the morning. Remember it has to be plain water without honey or lime or anything else, the first thing in the morning, as soon as you get up. Water triggers what is now scientifically called the gastrocolic reflex that stimulates your bowels. Over a period of time, it can correct poor bowel habits, which go a long way in keeping you healthy.
- Water helps your kidneys function properly: Our kidneys perform a few critical functions in the body. These include removing waste from our blood, balancing body fluids, and creating urine. Without water, our kidneys are unable to function properly.
- Water is the way to a clean gut: Water significantly aids in digestion. Your body uses water to break down and absorb water-soluble fats and fibre and move food through your body. If you are not hydrated enough, it

takes water from other sources in your body. Lack of water can actually increase your chances of constipation, leaving you uncomfortable and bloated. In fact, water can actually reduce the incidence of ulcers, bloating, gas, gastritis, acid reflux and irritable bowel. However, do not drink water along with or immediately after meals. A well-hydrated body purges toxins and metabolic wastes better.

- Weight management: Water will keep you full throughout the day. Often the sensation of hunger that we feel is actually a sensation of thirst. Confusing the two is very easy for the brain and this leads to us eating instead of drinking. So the next time you feel like eating at odd hours, try drinking water instead. Water boosts your metabolic rate and can help maximise your weight loss efforts. It also cleanses your body of waste and acts as an appetite suppressant. Drinking half a litre of water can increase metabolism by 24-30 per cent for up to an hour-and-a-half. This means that drinking two litres of water every day can increase your total energy expenditure by up to 96 calories per day.
- Water retention: Increase of excess fluid can have severe consequences including belly bloating, swollen ankles, nausea, cough and fatigue. Sometimes fluid build-up can rapidly escalate into a life-threatening situation. Contrary to what people think, drinking more water results in less fluid retention. Why? Because it helps the body to get rid of excess sodium that causes fluid retention in the first place.

- Blood pressure and cholesterol: When the body is fully hydrated, human blood is around 92 per cent water. This helps keep the blood moving freely without viscosity through the veins and arteries. This also prevents high blood pressure and other cardiovascular ailments. Low water intake makes the body produce more cholesterol to ensure that cells can function properly.
- Physical performance: Water helps to maximise your body's physical performance. Did you know that losing as little as two per cent of your body's water content can significantly impair your physical performance? Athletes can lose up to 6-10 per cent of their water weight due to sweating. This can lead to altered body temperature control, increased fatigue and can also make it difficult both physically and mentally to exercise. When muscle cells do not get adequate fluids, they don't function properly and this hits performance level. Water is an internal air conditioner—regulating body temperature through sweating and respiration.
- Water helps lubricate your joints, too: Most of our cartilage is composed of water, so if we don't consume enough, our bones feel stiffer and our joints take a beating.
- Kidney stones: Increased water intake appears to decrease the risk of kidney stone formation because it increases the volume of urine passing through the kidneys. This dilutes the concentration of minerals so that they are less likely to crystallise and form clumps.
- Headaches and migraines: Headaches can also be

indicative of dehydration. If you feel a headache coming and you know that you haven't had water for long, grab a glass of water immediately. Dehydration is often a cause for migraine and people prone to migraines must make an extra effort to keep their water intake regular. Only if the pain is intolerable, take a painkiller. However, remember that this will only treat the symptom and not the cause. Consult your doctor if your headache persists.

- Allergies and asthma: When our bodies are dehydrated they create more histamines—organic nitrous compounds that usually regulate our immune response. Increased histamine count can result in breathing difficulties and allergic reactions.
- Skin complexion: Water improves your skin complexion by moisturising your skin, and keeping it fresh, soft, glowing and smooth. It can help you in getting rid of early wrinkles. In fact, it is probably the best anti-aging treatment. You can reduce acne, dermatitis, psoriasis and premature aging through increased water consumption. Without water, our skin is unable to properly rid itself of toxins which results in the skin becoming irritated or inflamed.
- Mood booster: People who consume more water tend to have better moods. One particular study found that simply increasing your intake of water from 1.2 litres to 2.5 litres per day can result in less confusion, bewilderment, tiredness and drowsiness. The reverse is also true. People who usually consume two to four litres of water per day when restricted to one litre per

day find that they experience negative effects on their moods, including lower contentedness, calmness and/or positive emotions.
- Mental performance: The human brain is comprised of about 75 per cent water. People who drink water during cognitive tasks tend to perform better than those who do not. This applies to both adults and children. Even mild dehydration seems to impair cognitive function in the short term.
- Disease prevention: Proper hydration can prevent many health complications and diseases. Water consumption can protect against kidney stones, constipation, asthma, urinary tract infections, coronary heart disease and even some cancers.
- Slowing aging: All our organs require substantial amounts of water to function adequately. Staying dehydrated means that every cell, organ and system has to work harder. Net result, we age faster.

How much water should you be drinking?

Now, the big question: how much water should you drink in a day? The quantity of water you need to drink every day is impacted by various factors like:

- How much you exercise
- The climate (hot weather or high altitudes)
- Your general health (if you are diabetic for example, your body needs more fluids)
- If you're pregnant or breastfeeding.

If your health is normal, it is recommended that women should have about two litres or eight glasses of water a day and men should aim for at least three litres or twelve glasses a day. Keep track of your water intake during the day by leaving a water bottle in a spot that you can see throughout the day. Ensure that it is fully consumed by a target time.

It is possible that your water intake may be too much if you have certain health conditions such as thyroid disease, liver problems, kidney or heart issues. You may also need to control your water intake if you're taking medicines that cause water retention, for example, nonsteroidal anti-inflammatory drugs, opiate pain medications, and even some antidepressants. If you have a pre-existing medical condition, you should check with your doctor to ensure that you are getting the right amount of water each day.

Quality of water

We know that not drinking the right quantity of water can leave us dehydrated. However, did you know that not drinking the right quality of water can be harmful as well? Getting good quality water might not be as simple as buying the fanciest-looking mineral water bottle at the grocery store. There's a good chance that the water you're drinking is bad for you.

Bottled water and the water that undergoes the process of reverse osmosis—called RO water—mostly has salt content less than 50 parts per million (ppm). This is much below the Bureau of Indian Standards norm of 300 ppm and the World

Health Organisation's norm of 500 ppm. Salt depletion is associated with muscle cramps and a continuous supply of low salts in water is one of the causes of weakening heart muscles that can eventually lead to seizure or cramps in heart muscles.

You cannot replenish the salts provided by water by consuming vegetables or other foods. Absorption of salts by the body in liquid form is the most efficient as proven by science. In a scientific study performed to see if minerals consumed in food can make up for the lack of minerals in RO water, it was concluded that reduced mineral intake from water was not compensated by your diet. In fact, low-mineral water was responsible for an increased elimination of minerals from the body. In another chapter, we will discuss the acid-alkaline balance of the body and what you can do to make water more alkaline.

Remember that there is more to healthy water than lack of toxins. RO water seems to even leach minerals from the body. What this means is that the minerals we consume through food along with vitamins are being urinated away. Consumption of RO water leads to the dilution of electrolytes dissolved in the body's water. In fact, inadequate body water redistribution may even compromise the function of vital organs. A grandma remedy from Indian ayurveda is lime water with a pinch of salt. Alternatively, chamomile, asparagus and mulethi are supplements that help hydration.

Furthermore, did you know that mineral water sold in plastic bottles can often be harmful to your health, especially when exposed to heat for a prolonged period of time. When we go out for long drives, most of us carry a bottle of water with us, especially during summer. However, you do not always finish the water once the bottle is opened. You leave it in the car and drink it after a few hours, maybe even the next day. This is very dangerous to health due to the chemical 'biphenyl A' in plastic bottles. Although low levels of biphenyl A are relatively harmless, they are likely to increase when plastic is exposed to temperatures of 70 degrees Celsius or above. If the car is parked under the sun, the internal temperatures are likely to go up to 78 degrees Celsius. If you drink the water left in the car during this time, it is likely to affect your health adversely. It can also cause breast cancer, as high levels of dioxin is released when the heat reacts with the plastic of the bottle.

It is therefore recommended to always carry fresh water when you are going for a drive. You can carry a glass or metal bottle and refill it whenever required.

What can you do to make sure you are drinking water that is safe and not low in minerals? Filter running tap water with a clean cloth and boil it before drinking. Boiling is a reliable way to purify water. You can even use good quality water filters but remember that treated water might not be suitable for pregnant women and has an aftertaste that you might not like. So, whether or not you treat water, boiling it before drinking is still a safer and certainly a better alternative to RO water.

Water is a precious resource and must be treated thus. There's around 326 trillion gallons of water on earth. Of this, only 3 per cent is fresh water. Of this, 1.6 per cent is in the polar ice caps and glaciers while another 0.36 per cent is underground in aquifers and wells. That leaves a little over 1 per cent as the actual availability through the earth's lakes, rivers, streams and ponds. Treasure it.

KEY TAKEAWAYS

- Your body should be a reflection of the Earth. Adult bodies should be at least 70 per cent water.

- If you experience dry mouth, thirst, headaches, dizziness, drowsiness or constipation, then these are possible signs of dehydration.

- Water helps your body detox, ensures that your kidneys function properly, cleans your gut, promotes weight loss, reduces water retention, regulates blood pressure and cholesterol, lubricates your joints, reduces allergies and headaches, reduces instances of kidney stones, improves mood, slows ageing, improves mental performance and improves skin condition and complexion.

- You should aim to drink two to three litres of water per day.

- Quality of water is as important as quantity. Use filtered and boiled water instead of RO water.

STEP THREE: NOURISH

Mark Twain once joked that the only way to keep your health is to eat what you don't want, drink what you don't like and do what you would rather not. Of course, Mark Twain was being facetious. But just think about what Hippocrates, the Greek physician and the father of medicine, said: *food is medicine.* He believed that eating good food was the foundation for good health. 'Let food be thy medicine and medicine be thy food,' said Hippocrates.

The nineteenth century inventor Alexander Wolcott quipped, 'All the things I really like to do are either illegal, immoral, or fattening.' Witty, but rings true. The truth is that we are what we eat. This essentially means that eating healthy ensures good health. However, when one says 'eating healthy', what exactly does it mean?

One of my patients, a sixteen-year-old young girl, and an aspiring model, recently told me that she wanted to be size zero. She crash-dieted and deprived herself of a wholesome diet. This, for her, is healthy, as she feels there is no gain without pain. Is that your definition of being healthy as well? Then let me tell you that eating healthy is neither about crash diets nor is it about depriving yourself of foods you like. Following unhealthy trends blindly to reach your unrealistic goals does more harm than good to you.

Balanced diet

There is an old joke that goes, 'Eat, drink and be merry, for tomorrow you may diet.' It's a funny line but beautifully captures the fact that diets are anything but merry. But do diets need to be that way? No, no, no! Eating healthy simply means having a balanced diet.

What exactly is a balanced diet? A balanced diet is one that gives our body the nutrients it needs to function correctly. The food that we eat should not increase the toxin load on our bodies, should help to maintain mental clarity and poise and should not tax or burden our bodies. Essentially, a balanced diet means eating a variety of foods that provide you with essential nutrients like proteins, carbohydrates, fat, water, vitamins and minerals that you need to stay healthy, feel good, and have energy. To achieve this, one should consume a majority of our daily calories through fresh fruits, fresh vegetables, whole grains, legumes, nuts and lean proteins.

If you are amongst those who want to either lose weight or eat healthy in order to maintain a healthy weight, make sure you eat the right food. Remember that a balanced diet does not mean cutting down your fat intake drastically. In fact, if you are looking to lose weight, remember that simply cutting down fat from your diet is not the solution. Some fats are essential for you and not including them in your diet will do more harm than good. Plant-based fats like olive oil and those in avocados and nuts are healthy and extra satiating. Eat them instead of low-fat diets. The pun goes—dieting is wishful shrinking. True, but the shrinking should involve thinking closely about your diet. Also, do not be obsessed about your weight. Frankly, keeping track of your waist measurements in addition to your weight is a far better option.

Popular diet trends

If you feel weighed down by all the conflicting nutrition and diet advice out there, you are not alone. You will find that for every person who tells you that a certain food item is good for you, there is another one saying exactly the opposite. Over the past few decades, we have seen a slew of diets becoming popular. Some notable ones are:

- Atkins Diet: People on the Atkins diet avoid carbohydrates but can eat as much protein and fat as they like, particularly meat. This lowers their insulin and results in fat burn. However, drastically cutting carbs in the early phase of the programme can result in side-effects like headache, dizziness, weakness, fatigue and constipation.
- Ketogenic Diet: This involves reducing carbohydrate intake and upping fat intake. While it may sound contrary to common sense, it allows the body to burn stored fat as a fuel rather than sugar. In the beginning of

this diet, you may experience some negative symptoms, collectively referred to as 'low-carb flu' or 'keto flu' because they resemble the symptoms of flu. These may include headache, fatigue, increased hunger, diarrhoea, poor sleep, nausea, decreased physical performance and brain fog.

- South Beach Diet: This is not a traditional low-carb diet and instead focuses on selecting the right carbohydrates that have a lower glycemic index. It is considered to be safe if followed right. However, if you severely restrict your carbohydrates intake, you may experience the same problems as in the keto diet.
- Mediterranean Diet: This diet codifies the nutritional habits of the people of Crete, Greece and southern Italy. The emphasis is on plant foods, fresh fruits, beans, nuts, whole grains, seeds, olive oil, cheese, yoghurt, fish and poultry. There are no proven studies indicating the harmful side effects of this type of a diet, as it does not recommend fasting, starving or severely restricting yourself from certain type of food or nutrients. However, you should ensure that you get all the nutrients in recommended quantities through your diet.
- Fasting Diet: This requires intermittent fasting to lower insulin levels. Intermittent fasting can be for sixteen hours, eighteen hours, twenty-four hours or even a few days. There is a contrary view that eating breakfast within one hour of waking up is important to kick start your metabolism which intermittent fasting prevents. There is also a view that your body's muscle content

will decrease and your metabolism will suffer if you continue this diet for long.
- Weight Watchers Diet: People following this plan are not restricted to specific foods. Instead, a point system is used to monitor the daily diet. For example, an egg is worth 2 points and one tablespoon of olive oil is worth 1 point. While Weight Watchers focuses on counting points, not calories, counting calories is important. If you consume calories significantly below the average intake of 2,000 calories per day, you bear the risk of undernourishment.
- Raw Food Diet: This diet focuses on foods and drinks that are unprocessed, plant-based and usually organic. Many raw foodists are also vegans and do not eat or drink anything that is animal-based. People might experience mild headaches, cravings and nausea a few days after starting a diet of raw foods. These are some reactions from detoxification by raw foods.
- Vegetarian Diet: There are various types of vegetarians including lacto-vegetarian, fruitarian vegetarian, lacto-ovo vegetarian, living food diet vegetarian, ovo-vegetarian, pesco-vegetarian and semi-vegetarian. It is unimportant to get into the specifics of each variant here. Some might argue that a vegetarian diet lacks proteins. But soya is a rich source of protein. Adding soya in your diet will take care of your complete protein requirement.

In my opinion, the best person to know what suits your body and what doesn't is *you*. About 200 years ago, the founder of homeopathy, Dr Samuel Hahnemann, came up with a concept of a personalised or individualised diet. He was against the concept of a universal diet for everyone. Hahnemann said, 'Every man's stomach is like his foot.' Like one size of shoe does not fit all, one universal diet is not meant for all. Diet needs to be individualised depending on the needs and the digestive power of every individual. If you do not know your body, nobody else will.

If at all you need advice, please consult a nutrition expert. Under no circumstances should you opt for crash diets. When inclined to do so, please remember the words of the American comedian Totie Fields who said, 'I've been on a diet for two weeks and all I've lost is fourteen days.'

Crashing with crash diets

An unattributed quote goes something like, 'I'm on a seafood diet. I see food and I eat it.' Those who are unrestrained eaters often use crash diets as a possible solution. But crash diets are the most restrictive means of weight loss, as they involve severely cutting back on calories. These diets are meant for quick, short-term weight loss, which is not good for health in a broader perspective. Why? Because when you crash diet, your body will not be able to get the key nutrients that it needs for optimal health. If long-term deficiencies persist, it may lead to loss of minerals from your bones resulting in osteoporosis and easy fractures or loss of iron from the blood, leading to anaemia. In addition, low-calorie diets can lead to a deficiency in sodium and potassium, which may cause an increased risk of heart attack.

Crash diets also affect your mental and emotional health, often leaving dieters irritable, tired and lethargic. One can also slip into depression or develop eating disorders, such as anorexia and bulimia. Therefore, if you really want to lose weight without compromising with your health, then find out what is causing you to be overweight. Weight gain may be the result of some medical problems such as thyroid or polycystic ovarian syndrome among others. It is always better to take professional advice of a doctor or a nutritionist instead of depending on the word-of-mouth of a friend or the Internet.

Sense and moderation

Bollywood actress Kareena Kapoor took the media by storm with her miraculous weight loss through diet. It was the renowned dietician and nutritionist Rujuta Diwekar who supervised her weight-loss programme. Kareena says, 'I eat only simple Indian home food—sabzi, roti, dal, chawal, ghee. There are so many benefits of having ghee.' Having ghee is a piece of grandmotherly advice that is back in fashion after having been demonised for many decades.

Orson Welles famously quipped, 'Ask not what you can do for your country. Ask what's for lunch.' Increasingly, that seems to be a good rule to live by—eating lunch like a king. Jane Fonda says, 'I skip dinner whenever possible. I eat a really big, wholesome breakfast, a good lunch around three or four p.m., and no dinner,' says the Oscar-winning actress and fitness icon.

Think about the junk that we consume daily. Actor Akshay Kumar likes his food as natural as possible. He says, 'I don't eat things that are made in a lab. I eat brown rice. It is good for your muscles as it is good carb. I eat a lots of walnuts, cranberries, almond, and milk. Avoid processed foods.'

What do all the above examples tell us? Simple, really. The answer to good nutrition lies in two words: sense and moderation.

Let me give you a real life example of how habits can change lives:

Twenty-four-year-old Vineeta was fighting obesity for a long time. Her parents were worried because it was time for her to settle down in life and they thought she would not be able to find a suitable life partner because she was overweight. Vineeta tried a low-fat diet to lose weight but it only brought temporary results. Around the same time, she met a nutritionist and thought of taking her advice on what to eat in order to lose weight, instead of depending on tips from the Internet and other unreliable sources. Vineeta followed her nutritionist's advice and the results were fabulous.

What did her nutritionist tell her? Two simple tips. First, to give her refrigerator a total makeover. She told Vineeta what she needed in her fridge and what she should get rid of. Surprisingly, the first thing she had to get rid of were her low-fat snacks. Second, to keep an apple with her always and to remember that if she were truly hungry, then an apple would seem delicious. If it didn't, she was not hungry. If hunger wasn't the problem, then food wasn't the solution. Just sipping some green tea or warm water would do the trick. 'A diet is the penalty we pay for exceeding the feed limit,' joked her nutritionist.

Vineeta followed her nutritionist's instructions diligently. She gave her refrigerator a completely new look by placing fruits and vegetables inside clear containers. She placed them along with yogurt and healthy salads on a shelf at eye level. Now when she opened the door of her refrigerator, healthy food would grab her attention. She also threw out takeaway containers because they only encouraged her to eat the wrong food. As a result, Vineeta made healthier choices. Also, she followed a balanced diet, which included the right amount of proteins, iron and even healthy fats that made her feel full instead of low fat foods that made her feel deprived. The apple trick worked wonderfully for her, as with it she knew when she was hungry. When she was, she just ate an apple! With these two simple changes, she dropped four kilos in a month's time.

According to the National Health and Medical Research Council (NHMRC) of Australia, you should be eating from the five major groups of foods as shown on p. 36:

How you eat is as important as what you eat

People often eat while watching television or while engaging on their mobiles. Research suggests that eating when you're distracted results in consuming many extra calories in a day. So, sit down whenever you eat, preferably at a table. Turn off the television or computer and put down your phone. Look at your food and smell it. Chew slowly, and don't take another bite until you have chewed enough.

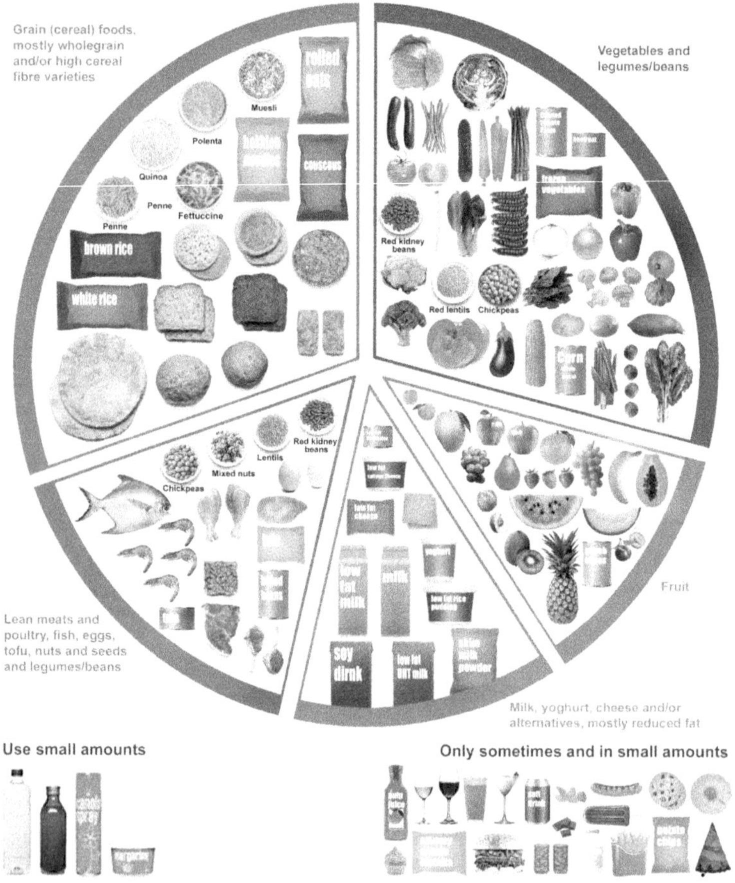

Grain (cereal) foods, mostly wholegrain and/or high cereal fibre varieties

Vegetables and legumes/beans

Fruit

Milk, yoghurt, cheese and/or alternatives, mostly reduced fat

Lean meats and poultry, fish, eggs, tofu, nuts and seeds and legumes/beans

Use small amounts

Only sometimes and in small amounts

Here are some creative tips to eating better:

- Chew every morsel of your food thirty-two times. Our Indian grandmothers would say in Hindi, '*Daanton se khao, aanton se nahin.*' It meant that the work of chewing should be done by the teeth, not the intestines.
- Eat your last meal before 6.30 p.m. if possible. If not, eat it at the earliest that you can, keeping a gap of minimum three hours in between your last meal and sleeping.
- Try to get the maximum amount of your nutrition from completely unprocessed foods. This not only means more fruit and vegetables but also means brown rice instead of white rice and whole grains instead of refined grains. It's better to consume two apples rather than consuming a glass of apple juice. Moderately processed foods—such as pasta—should be consumed less. Heavily processed foods should be the least consumed. This includes bread, chips, cookies and cereals.
- Don't exchange your healthy food for unhealthy stuff.
- Avoid empty calories i.e. any food or drink that has zero nutritional value besides its energy value. Items included in this bucket are sugary drinks, sweets and most breakfast cereals. The cartoonist Robert Thaves once joked, 'Inside me there is a thin person struggling to get out but I usually sedate him with four or five cupcakes.' High sugar and high carb foods are only temporary relief from cravings.
- Don't eat fruits and nuts after 4 p.m. These are difficult to digest and place a load on your digestive system.

Remember, the digestive system works best between 10 a.m and 4 p.m.
- It takes a few minutes for your brain to get a signal that you are full. Eat slowly so that there is enough time for your brain to receive information from your stomach. If you simply stop for a few minutes to let your food settle, you will be more capable of stopping. Remember that there is a distinction between need and greed.
- Whenever possible, cook meals at home. This makes it far easier to avoid processed ingredients and gives you far more control over what you eat. Use salt and fats, including butter and oil, as required. Stop treating them as enemies.
- Moderation is everything. One of the easy ways of getting yourself to eat in moderation is to divide your plate into quarters. Half your plate (two quarters) should be occupied by fruits and vegetables. Another quarter of the plate should be covered by protein, and the final quarter can be carbs or starches such as bread, rice, baked potato or pasta.
- Find out if you are an emotional eater. Overeating can be a way of pushing down unwanted feelings. Try to have control on your emotions. Stay happy. Look at other areas of your life. Do you have a sense of purpose? Do you really enjoy your job and your personal life? If something is bothering you, you might tend to eat the wrong stuff at the wrong times.
- Choose eating-out options wisely. In particular, avoid fast food joints.

- Medicines might make you fat. The intake of certain medicines causes weight gain. These include steroids and oral contraceptive pills. Discuss the possibilities for reducing your dose with your doctor if you want to lose weight.
- Drink lots of water through the day. Some alcohol, coffee or other beverages are fine. Again, moderation is important. If you use dear old Google-baba, you will find articles for and against everything.
- Total abstinence can rarely be followed through in perpetuity. There is no need to make any food or beverage taboo. Keep aside one meal per week as a 'cheat meal'. But again, even with cheat meals, don't go overboard.
- A balanced internal ecosystem is vital to the well-being of your gut. Consider consuming a probiotic supplement and eating fibre-rich foods to keep your gut clean. Most ailments can be traced back to a gut that is in disrepair.
- Do not be affected by what people say about you. There is a joke that defines the word 'unhealthy' as 'what thin people call you when you're fat and what fat people call you when you're thin'. Be sensible in your eating habits for yourself, not others.
- Always look at the nutrition information on packages. Some items that claim to be 'reduced fat' or 'fat-free' may contain extra sodium, sugar or other chemicals that can be bad for your body.

- Maintain an acid-alkaline balance in what you eat. Your plate should have two-thirds alkaline and one-third acidic food (refer to the chart on pg. 51 to know which foods are acidic and which are alkaline).

Going organic

The comedian Robert Orben joked that older people shouldn't eat health food because they need all the preservatives they can get. But preservatives do precisely the opposite. They preserve the food but do little to preserve you. Who was the wise guy who said, 'I used to eat a lot of natural foods until I learned that most people die of natural causes'?

Organic food has become popular today. However, do you really know what organic food is? Is organic food really better for your mental and physical health? The chart below from helpguide.org can assist you in understanding organic food better and how it is different from non-organic conventionally grown stuff.

	Organic	**Conventional**
Produce	Grown with natural fertilisers (manure, compost)	Grown with synthetic or chemical fertilisers
	Weeds are controlled naturally (crop rotation, hand weeding, mulching and tilling)	Weeds are controlled with chemical herbicides

	ACIDIC				ALKALINE		
	Most Acidic	Acidic	Least Acidic		Least Alkaline	Alkaline	Most Alkaline
Sweeteners	Nutra Sweet, Equal, Aspartame, Sweet 'n Low	White sugar, brown sugar	Processed honey, molasses		Raw honey, raw sugar	Maple syrup, rice syrup	Stevia
Fruits	Blueberries, cranberries, prunes	Sour cherries, rhubarb	Plums, processed fruit juices		Oranges, bananas, cherries, pineapple, peaches, avocados	Dates, figs, melons, grapes, papaya, kiwi, berries, apples, pears, raisins	Lemons, watermelon, limes, grapefruit, mangoes, papaya
Beans, Vegetables, Legumes	Chocolate	Potatoes without skin, pinto beans, navy beans,	Cooked spinach, kidney beans, string beans		Carrots, tomatoes, fresh corn, mushrooms,	Okra, squash, green beans, beets, celery, lettuce,	Asparagus, onions, vegetable juices,

	ACIDIC			ALKALINE		
	Most Acidic	Acidic	Least Acidic	Least Alkaline	Alkaline	Most Alkaline
		Lima beans		cabbage, peas, potato skins, olives, soybeans, tofu	zucchini, sweet potato	parsley, raw spinach, broccoli, garlic
Nuts, Seeds	Peanuts, walnuts	Pecans, cashews	Pumpkin seeds, sunflower seeds	Chestnuts	Almonds	
Oils Grains, Cereals	Wheat, white flour, pastries, pasta	White rice, corn, buckwheat, oats, rye	Corn oil sprouted wheat bread, spelt, brown rice	Canola oil amaranth, millet, wild rice, quinoa	Flax seed oil	Olive oil
Meats, Poultry, Fish	Beef, pork, shellfish	Turkey, chicken, lamb	Venison, cold water fish			

	ACIDIC			ALKALINE		
	Most Acidic	Acidic	Least Acidic	Least Alkaline	Alkaline	Most Alkaline
Eggs, Dairy	Cheese, homogenised milk, ice-cream	Raw milk	Eggs, butter, yoghurt, buttermilk, cottage cheese	Soy cheese, soy milk, goat milk, goat cheese, whey		
Beverages	Beer, soft drinks	Coffee	Tea	Ginger tea	Green tea	Herb teas, lemon water

	Organic	**Conventional**
	Pests are controlled using natural methods (birds, insect traps) and naturally-derived pesticides.	Pests are controlled with synthetic pesticides.
Meat, dairy and eggs	Livestock are given all organic, hormone-free and GMO-free feed.	Livestock are given growth hormones for faster growth, as well as non-organic, GMO feed.
	Disease is prevented with natural methods such as clean housing, rotational grazing and healthy diet.	Antibiotics and medications are used to prevent livestock disease.
	Livestock must always have access to the outdoors.	Livestock may or may not have access to the outdoors.

What are the benefits of organic food? There are several.

- Organic produce is safe, as it does not contain chemicals such as fungicides, herbicides and insecticides.
- Organic food is often fresher as it does not contain preservatives.
- Organic farming is better for the environment.
- Organic meat and milk are richer in certain nutrients.

Food can act like medicine. If you get your diet right, you probably may not need any medicines. What you feed your body becomes the foundation for good health. If food has the power to prevent many chronic illnesses, doesn't it make sense to alter our diets to use food to our own advantage?

Going vegan

It's becoming quite trendy and fashionable to be vegan nowadays and many celebrities globally are supporting this trend. However, there is much more to a vegan diet than celebrity endorsements. When you switch to vegan diet, what you basically do is eliminate meat and animal products from your diet. Vegans consume a diet rich in whole foods, such as fruits, vegetables, whole grains, legumes, nuts and seeds.

When followed the right way, this diet may result in various health benefits, including a trimmer waistline and improved blood sugar control. Natural plant-based diet is rich in fibre, folic acid, vitamins C and E, magnesium, unsaturated fat and phytochemicals. Vegans therefore have low risk of high cholesterol and blood pressure, obesity and heart disease. Almonds, chickpeas, broccoli, lentils, spinach and tofu are all rich in proteins. Soya is as rich a source of proteins as meat and offers you nutrients that meat lacks. The problem however is that most people have no idea what's in their food.

Do you think that the steak that you eat is a rich source of fibre? You are in for a surprise then. Steak has no fibre at all! By definition, fibre is only found in plants. There is no fibre in meat, dairy or eggs, and little or no fibre in junk food.

While meat lacks fibre, soya is extremely rich in fibre. Fibre to a great extent helps in weight loss.

Veganism is not only about loving animals, but about loving yourself, too

Just looking into the eyes of a goat, a pig or any other animal on the way to a slaughter house or watching any video on the way animals are slaughtered will put you off meat forever. However, veganism is not only about loving animals but also about loving yourself. Being vegan can keep you away from many infections. Several microbes that cause ailments in human beings are becoming resistant to antibiotics. One of the reasons for this is an excessive use of antibiotics by the meat industry, which frequently feeds antibiotics to livestock animals from birth to slaughter to promote growth. Also, did you know that the animals that you eat aren't fed what they're designed to eat? They are fed something that is cheap and makes them grow faster. Many might not know but animals are sometimes fed boiled and ground up remains of dead (sometimes even diseased) animals.

If you insist on a warm glass of milk every morning for your child, thinking it is one of the best things you are doing for his health, here's something that could make you look at the glass half empty. Cattle in many cattle houses across the country are injected with a banned hormone called oxytocin every day. While the drug forces the cattle to expel a few extra litres of milk, studies have indicated the consumption of milk contaminated with oxytocin is linked to the early onset of puberty in children, which is on an alarming rise these days.

Also, if hormone or antibiotics injections are administered twice every day to animals, as is the current practice, the drug stays in the milk and the meat, and causes serious ailments like breast cancer and prostate cancer, also impotency in men.

Furthermore, eggs and cow's milk are amongst common causes of allergies in infants and the most common animal food allergens in adults are fish and other seafood. Also, did you know that the fish you eat might be adulterated with formalin, an anti-decomposition agent used as a germicide, fungicide and disinfectant for fish? Extreme exposure to formalin can increase your risk of suffering from various kinds of cancer. Initially, formalin intake can cause diarrhoea, vomiting and upset stomach. In the long run, it can have adverse effects on kidney, liver and skin.

Tennis champ Venus Williams said in one of her interviews to *Health* that she switched to a raw vegan diet after being diagnosed with an autoimmune disorder. 'Once I started, I fell in love with the concept of fuelling your body in the best way possible. Not only does it help me on the court, but I feel like I'm doing the right thing for me. It definitely changed my whole life,' she said.

Some other celebrities who have made the commitment to banish meat and dairy from their lives are Ariana Grande, Miley Cyrus, Madonna, Jennifer Lopez, Mayim Bialik,

Russell Simmons, Pamela Anderson, James Cameron, Alicia Silverstone and Serena Williams, amongst others.

Having said that, what is more important is making sure you get the right amount of nutrients. It is recommended that you keep your physician in the loop about your eating habits and ensure you are meeting all the requirements for good health.

The fuss about artificial sweeteners and sodas

With fifteen to twenty calories per teaspoon, a small amount of regular sugar can be a part of anyone's healthy diet. However, if you are replacing it with artificial sweetneners in an attempt to lose weight or control blood sugar levels, you might be causing more harm to your body than good.

Artificial sweeteners may change the way you taste your food, due to which you are less likely to make healthier food choices. Routine use of artificial sweeteners can make you shun healthy and nutritious foods while consuming more artificially flavoured foods with less nutritional value. This happens because frequent use of these 'hyper-intense' sweeteners leads to overstimulation of sugar receptors. This means people who routinely use them may find foods that are not intensely sweet, like fruits, less appealing, and foods such as vegetables downright unpalatable!

Studies indicate that daily consumption of artificial sweeteners was associated with a 36 per cent greater risk for metabolic syndrome (abdominal obesity, high blood pressure and high blood sugar) and a 67 per cent increased risk for type-2 diabetes. Aren't these diseases that artificial sweeteners claim to help prevent in the first place?

You may argue saying you could give up these sweeteners whenever you want. However, there are certain studies that indicate that artificial sweeteners may be addictive and it may be difficult for you to stop their use if you have been taking them for a prolonged time.

When it comes to having so-called diet foods and beverages, check the ingredient lists. Understand that low-fat is not no-fat. Diet soda may contain aspartame, which according to some studies might cause cancer with long-term use. Also, many of these diet drinks contain caffeine, which may curb your appetite temporarily, but may lead to overeating later on in the day. Sodas also contain phosphorus, too much of which can leech calcium from your bones, weakening them. Also, understand that with sodas you may bloat easily since they often cause indigestion. So, why not replace colas with water? Adequate water intake flushes toxins from our kidneys and helps us to lose weight. It is also free of calories!

If at all you have to use artificial sweeteners, opt for natural stevia. Unlike other sugar substitutes, stevia is derived from a plant and a safer alternative to sugar.

Someone has joked, 'An apple a day keeps the doctor away. An onion a day takes care of everyone else.' Both the apple and the onion have important nutritional value for us. The key lies in having a little of everything.

Key Takeaways

- Food is vital in ensuring good health.
- Follow a balanced diet rather than a crash diet. A balanced diet is one that gives your body all the nutrients it needs to function correctly.
- The answer to good nutrition lies in two words: sense and moderation.
- Your daily diet should include items like grains, vegetables, legumes and fruit.
- How you eat is as important as what you eat. Eat slowly.
- Eat your last meal at least three hours before turning in.
- Try to get maximum nutrition from unprocessed foods, preferably organic. Cooking at home is better than eating out.
- Maintain an acid-alkaline balance. Use a natural probiotic, if necessary.

STEP FOUR: MOVE

The dean of Yale Law School, Robert M. Hutchins, once joked, 'Whenever I feel like exercise, I lie down until the feeling passes.' Are you like that too? Let me convince you why you should change your ways.

We all know that exercise is good for us, but do we know how good it *actually* is? Most of us think that exercise only aids weight loss. However, there is much more to it than just helping you lose weight. From boosting your mood to improving your sex life, exercise has a lot of positive benefits. Regular exercise can even protect you from several chronic diseases. Exercise is defined as any movement that makes your muscles—including your heart—work, and thus requires your body to burn calories.

Did you know that our bodies are meant to move? The human body actually craves exercise since humans were originally hunter-gatherers. That is the reason it suffers when we have sedentary lifestyles. Regular exercise is not only necessary for physical fitness but also for mental fitness. What's more, it can improve your appearance and delay aging. Exercise makes you less prone to illnesses and reduces the risk of many critical medical conditions. Let's examine some of the benefits of exercise.

Benefits of exercise

- Mood improvement: Former first lady, Michelle Obama, says: 'For me, exercise is more than just physical—it's therapeutic.' Studies have shown that exercise can improve your mood and reduce depression, anxiety and stress. Why and how does exercise make this happen? Exercise actually causes changes in those areas of the brain that control stress and anxiety. Exercise improves the sensitivity of your brain to hormones such as serotonin and norepinephrine. These are hormones that reduce feelings of depression. It also ups the manufacture of endorphins which boost positivity and reduce pain. Interesting is the fact that the intensity of your workout is not that important; even moderate exercise can act as an upper.
- Improved sleep: Increased fitness also improves sleep patterns. As little as ten minutes of aerobic exercise, such as walking or cycling, can dramatically improve the quality of your sleep, especially when done on a regular basis. Why? Because energy depletion that occurs during exercise stimulates recuperative processes during sleep. One study found that around 150 minutes of moderate-to-vigorous activity each week can bring about a 65 per cent improvement in sleep quality.
- Weight loss: Someone joked that the definition of aerobics is a series of exercises which help convert fats,

sugars and starches into aches, pains and cramps. Witty, but the truth is boring. Inactivity can be a significant factor in obesity. The human body expends energy in three main ways—digesting food; maintaining regular body functions such as beating of the heart and breathing; and finally, exercise. When you diet, your reduced calorie count lowers your metabolic rate. This would have the effect of not lowering your weight loss unless you exercise. A well-balanced plan of cardio and resistance training is ideal to compensate for that.

- Heart health: As you age, you suddenly find that simple activities like walking or carrying groceries become difficult. You experience fatigue, shortness of breath, fluid build-up, and coughing while carrying out these activities. Essentially your heart is not pumping as well as it should. Exercise can strengthen your heart. If you want to get the maximum benefit from exercise, you should aim to reach between 50-85 per cent of your maximum heart rate. Climbing stairs is one of the easiest ways to get into that target range. You can either do it at home or at the gym on a stair machine. To find your maximum heart rate, simply subtract your age from 220. Swimming, brisk walking, running, cycling and dancing are some of the activities that might help you to keep your heart healthy.
- Regulate blood sugar: If you have diabetes, exercise can help regulate your blood sugar level. Remaining fit and active can control your diabetes and keep your blood sugar level in the normal range. This is essential

to prevent long-term complications of diabetes such as nerve pain and kidney disease. If you are insulin resistant, exercise can make your insulin more effective.
- Fertility and libido: Exercise may improve your fertility if you are overweight. It also helps in cases where medical ailments like polycystic ovarian syndrome are the cause of infertility. Making exercise a part of your daily regime before trying to conceive can help you feel good throughout your pregnancy, have more stamina for labour and delivery, and shed the baby weight faster. Exercise enhances sexual desire, function and performance in both men and women. It also decreases the risk of erectile dysfunction in men.
- Posture and flexibility: Stretching exercises are important for good posture. They keep your body supple so that you can bend, reach and twist. Improving your flexibility through exercise reduces the chance of injury and improves balance and coordination. If you have stiff, tense areas such as the upper back or neck, performing specific stretches can help 'loosen' those muscles, helping you feel more relaxed. Low-impact aerobic activities can increase the strength and endurance of your back and also improve muscle function. Abdominal and back muscle exercises, which are core-strengthening exercises, may help reduce back pain symptoms by strengthening the muscles around your spine.
- Bone density and muscle tone: Exercise strengthens bones and also firms up muscles. Walking or skipping

helps maintain as well as improve bone density in people with low bone density or osteoporosis. Strengthening exercises—using weights or resistance bands—also help in maintaining or improving bone density at the location of the targeted muscle attachments. Weight training can accelerate muscle building when it is combined with increased protein intake because it releases hormones that promote muscular absorption of amino acids.

- Reduces asthma attacks: Regular exercise can also help control the frequency and severity of asthma attacks. In Montreal, Canada, researchers studied sixty-six adult asthmatics for twelve weeks in 2015. The asthmatics were divided into two groups—one that exercised and one that did not. The results showed that those in the exercise group had clinically and statistically significant improvements in asthma control. For instance, they used their rescue medicine far less on average than those in the control group.
- Reduced blood pressure and belly fat: Regular exercise has been shown to improve insulin sensitivity, cardiovascular fitness and body composition, while lowering blood pressure and blood fat levels. As against that, lack of regular exercise can increase belly fat which, in turn, increases the risk of type-2 diabetes and heart disease.
- Reduces arthritic pain: Exercise can reduce pain and help maintain muscle strength in affected joints and reduce joint stiffness, thereby providing relief from arthritis and related conditions.

- Brain health and memory: The English actor, Sir Norman Wisdom, once quipped, 'As you get older, three things happen. The first is your memory goes, and I can't remember the other two.' Maybe Sir Norman should have exercised more. Exercise can enhance brain function and protect memory and thinking skills. Exercise pumps up your heart rate which, in turn, enhances the flow of blood and oxygen to your brain. It also increases the production of hormones that can enhance the growth of brain cells. Exercise can combat the effects of aging, oxidative stress and inflammation. Exercise causes an increase in the size of the hippocampus, that part of the brain that's critical for memory and learning. Exercise has even been shown to reduce alterations in the brain caused by Alzheimer's and schizophrenia.
- Energy levels: The French author Jules Renard one joked, 'Laziness is nothing more than the habit of resting before you get tired.' But exercise can be a real energy booster for healthy people, as well as those suffering from various medical conditions. One study found that six weeks of regular exercise reduced feelings of fatigue for healthy people who had previously reported persistent fatigue. In fact, exercise can significantly increase energy levels for people suffering from chronic fatigue syndrome (CFS) and other serious illnesses. Exercise has even been shown to enhance energy levels in people suffering from progressive illnesses such as cancer, HIV/AIDS and multiple sclerosis.
- Skin health: Skin is influenced by the oxidative stress

in your body. Oxidative stress takes place when the body's antioxidant barriers are unable to completely repair damage caused by free radicals. Beware though. Intense physical activity can aggravate oxidative damage while regular and moderate exercise can up your body's natural antioxidants.

Four types of exercise

When we titled this chapter 'Move', we meant it. There are four basic types of movement that we need:

- Cardio exercise: Cardio is short for cardiovascular exercise. This means endurance exercise that fortifies your body's circulatory system—your heart and blood vessels. Examples of cardio include aerobics, running, working out on an elliptical trainer, biking, or even dancing.
- Strength training: As compared to cardio, strength training is exercise that uses resistance to contract muscles with the aim of increasing strength, enhancing anaerobic endurance, and strengthening your skeletal muscles. Examples are weight training, pilates and bodyweight exercises like push-ups, pull-ups, and sit-ups.
- Flexibility training: These are exercises to improve the flexibility and suppleness of your body. Yoga is a prime example of flexibility training. There are many trainers who lump yoga into the strength training category but as Sadhguru Jaggi Vasudev says, 'If you do a lot of weights,

your muscles will look big. You've seen people who have grown big muscles; they cannot do a namaskar properly. They cannot even bend.'
- 'Unsitting': American actress Phyllis Dyer once joked, 'My idea of exercise is a good brisk sit.' While the quip can get many laughs, the problem lies in sitting for extended periods. Unsitting simply means not allowing yourself to sit for too long because sitting is the new smoking. Sitting continuously at your desk can increase your risk of heart disease, diabetes, colon cancer, deep vein thrombosis and even dementia. Several step-counters and smart watches prompt you to stand and engage in some physical activity every hour to avoid medical problems. Some people are even installing treadmill desks that allow users to walk while working.

Exercise tips

Fine, so we know that exercise is good for us, but how much should we exercise? There have been enough commentators who have warned us about the perils of over-exercise. The TV show host Ellen DeGeneres wittily commented, 'My grandmother started walking five miles a day when sixty. She's ninety-seven now and we don't know where the hell she is!'

But you don't need to walk five miles a day. To maintain a healthy weight, it is suggested that you should perform some form of cardio or aerobic exercise at least three times a week for a minimum of twenty-five minutes. However, if you have to lose weight, then more is recommended. Incorporating just twenty-five minutes of moderate exercise—such as brisk walking—on a daily basis will burn up to 100 extra calories depending on your speed. However, make sure you do not consume excess calories in your diet afterwards. In all:

- Aim for at least thirty minutes of physical activity five times a week.
- See everyday activities as a good opportunity to be active.
- Try to find the time for some regular, vigorous exercise for extra health and fitness benefits.
- Minimise the amount of time spent in prolonged sitting and break up long periods of sitting as often as possible.
- Use a step monitor—it enables you to rack up extra steps (the goal should be 10,000 steps per day).

Make exercise time fun time

There are those of us who find an exercise regime boring. An unattributed wisecrack says, 'Eat right, exercise regularly, die anyway.' Ouch! Many of us find it difficult to stick to a particular exercise regime; others don't know where to start. The key to taking up or keeping to any form of physical activity is to have fun. Enjoy getting fit by following these few simple steps.

- Wake up the child within you: What types of activities did you enjoy when you were a kid? Did you enjoy playing a sport or dance? Give them a try again.

- Find an exercise buddy: It has been found that we are more likely to stick to physical activity if we do it with friends or family. So find an exercise buddy for you who will keep you on your toes always.
- Mix it up: Don't follow the same exercise routine every day. Try a variety of fun activities every day. Not only does a range of activities keep your interest up, they challenge different muscles. So play a sport, enjoy swimming, dance to your favourite music, take a walk with your friend or take your kids to a park and play with them.
- Take up the challenge: Keep up your interest by trying new activities. Go out trekking with friends or join a group for cycling or the marathon.

There are numerous cases documented by me that highlight how exercise can change lives. Take one example:

Nadira at the age of sixty-seven found it difficult to walk and was unable to sleep for more than four hours a day. She also experienced trembling and rigidity in her body movements. She was diagnosed with Parkinson's disease. It is a disorder where the nerve cells in the brain are affected leading to muscle rigidity, tremors, and changes in speech. Along with medical treatment, her doctor recommended regular brisk walking. Aerobic exercise enhances trophic factors—small proteins in the brain—that behave like fertilisers. They do to our bodies what fertilisers do to our lawn. Exercise thus helps maintain brain connections and counters brain shrinkage from Parkinson's disease as well as from brain aging. In Nadira's case, regular exercise helped her get symptomatic relief from Parkinson's disease.

Here's another:

Twenty-eight-year-old Vaishali wanted to have a child but was unable to conceive inspite of trying for two years. She and her husband underwent all the tests suggested by their physician. All their reports were absolutely normal. However, she was unable to conceive. They even changed doctors. Every time they went for a consultation they were asked to undergo some or the other test. Every test report was normal and yet Vaishali was unable to have a child. This made her feel that she would never be able to become a mother and this led to depression. She was diagnosed with primary infertility. On the recommendation of one of her family members she consulted a senior gynecologist. To her surprise, the doctor said, 'There is no need for any tests. Just follow two things and everything else will fall in place.' Vaishali was shocked to hear this. The two things her doctor suggested her to do were to exercise and lose some weight and destress herself. After following a strict exercise regime for around five months, Vaishali lost eight kilos. Exercise also helped her to balance her stress levels. Six months later she missed her period and her pregnancy test came positive. Today, Vaishali is the mother of a two-year-old boy and cannot thank her gynaecologist enough for giving her the 'guru mantra' on the importance of exercise.

And yet another:

Nimisha had never thought that a small accident—the twisting of an ankle while walking down the stairs—would lead to three broken bones, a three-hour surgery, three months of recovery period and about six months to get back to her normal routine! Only after it happened did she realise how much for granted we take our health, especially our bone health. After this incident she decided to strengthen her bones and the most effective way to achieve this was to follow a regular exercise regimen. Initially, Nimisha followed some simple physiotherapy exercises to get her ankle moving. It was followed by regular walks for thirty minutes a day. This developed her muscles, bones and ligaments and increased strength as well as endurance. Her posture improved as well and her muscles became firm and toned. Today, she has much stronger bones. She not only feels better, but is looking better too.

Hippocrates, who lived around 400 BC, recommended exercise. If you went to him complaining of any ailment he would tell you to exercise, eat healthy and bathe. If you didn't take his advice seriously, the alternative was to visit and pray at the Temple of Asclepius at Epidaurus. To reach there you would walk a lot anyway. In effect, you would be heeding his prescription. So what are you waiting for? Move!

Key Takeaways

- The human body actually craves exercise, since humans were originally hunter-gatherers.

- The benefits of exercise include mood improvement, better sleep, weight loss, cardio health, regulated blood sugar, higher fertility and libido, better posture and flexibility, better bone density and muscle tone, reduced asthma, reduced blood pressure and belly fat, reduced arthritic pain, improved brain health and memory, higher energy levels and improved skin.

- There are four key types of exercise—cardio, strength, flexibility and unsitting.

- Sitting is the new smoking. Avoid long stretches of sitting, even at work.

- Aim for at least thirty minutes of physical activity five times a week.

- Use a step monitor and aim for 10,000 steps per day.

STEP FIVE: DIGEST

The Greek physician Hippocrates is believed to have said, 'All disease begins in the gut.' It has taken us several centuries to realise the profound wisdom of what he said. The inside of your gut is like a buzzing township. Scientists estimate that we have 100 trillion bacteria living inside of us. That's about ten times the number of human cells we have. Incredible as it may sound, we are more bacteria than human!

Around 300 to 500 kinds of bacteria reside in the township called your gut. Collectively, they contain nearly two million genes. When coupled with other micro-organisms like fungi and viruses, they constitute the microbiota—or the microbiome. The gut is probably the most powerful organ in your body and your overall health—or lack of it—is closely linked to the happenings in your gut.

Over generations we have been taught that bacteria are to be avoided. We spend millions buying cleaning products to specifically eliminate bacteria. As it happens, our bodies are brimming with trillions of bacteria and they help digest food and play a vital role in our overall health. As research progresses, it is becoming clear that the wrong balance of gut bacteria is closely linked to conditions such as diabetes, obesity, depression and colon cancer.

All gut bacteria is not good. But that's not something to worry too much about. For good health, we only need 80 per cent of our gut bacteria to be good. The remaining 20 per cent can be bad. Thus, what we want is that 80-20 balance in gut bacteria.

How often have you heard someone say, 'My gut tells me that … ?' Your gut is indeed a voice and it often communicates in various ways—silence, rumbling, hunger pangs, acidic fires, loose motions or constipation, among others. The gut is ultimately responsible for breaking down and absorbing nutrients from the food we eat. This impacts everything, whether it is hormone balance, energy production, skin tone, mental well-being, toxin and waste elimination. It may surprise you to note that 70 per cent of the body's immune system is located in the gut.

What are gut bacteria?

Every individual human being's microbiota is unique—like a fingerprint or DNA. The unique cocktail of bacteria in your system is remarkably different to that of your parent, sibling or spouse. There are only two key factors that play a role in determining the mix: first, your mother's microbiota, essentially the womb environment that you were born into; second, your diet and lifestyle.

Bacteria, as we know, live throughout your body. But the ones in your gut have the greatest effect on your overall health. They line your digestive system, mostly living in your intestines and colon. They have a bearing on virtually everything from your metabolism to your mood.

Recent scientific studies seem to indicate that gut bacteria of healthy individuals are different from those who have certain health disorders. Sick individuals may actually have too much or too little of a given kind of bacteria. While some kinds of bacteria may protect against specific diseases, others may elevate the risk of those very ailments.

Linkages to diseases

Medical research has now begun to establish links between different types of illnesses and your gut bacteria. Here are some examples:

- Inflammatory bowel, irritable bowel, Crohn's disease and ulcerative colitis: These conditions are linked to deficiency of certain anti-inflammatory bacteria. In fact, it is believed that some bacteria may trick your body to attack your intestines thus laying the ground for inflammatory bowel, Crohn's disease or ulcerative colitis. Researchers have found that unbalanced gut bacteria is a leading cause of these conditions. Want proof? Increasingly, doctors are undertaking fecal transplants in which stool is donated by a healthy patient and placed into the colon of a sick patient. It sounds disgusting but surprisingly has a 93 per cent success rate in restoring bacterial balance and curing digestive issues.
- Obesity, type-2 diabetes, and heart disease: Your gut

bacteria definitely plays a role in your metabolism. Bacteria seems to determine how many calories you are able to draw from food and which specific nutrients you are able to absorb from it. An overload of gut bacteria can actually turn fibre into fatty acids leading to fat deposits in your liver. This condition is called 'metabolic syndrome' which often results in obesity, type-2 diabetes or heart disease. If you eat healthy, exercise and still struggle to lose weight, the reason probably lies in your gut bacteria.

- Anxiety, depression, autism: Your gut is full of nerve endings that regularly talk to your brain. Embedded in the walls of your intestine are 500 million neurons that constitute your enteric nervous system or ENS. Your ENS is responsible for regulating the production of thirty different neurotransmitters that regulate moods. This connection is often called the 'gut-brain axis' and this axis is often viewed as the link between gut bacteria and ailments of the central nervous system. These ailments include anxiety, depression and autism. Compromised digestion often results in lower production of neurotransmitters such as serotonin which is mostly produced in the small intestine. Low serotonin is an oft-cited cause of anxiety and depression. In case studies with mice, medical researchers were able to entirely alter the behaviour of mice by modifying the balance of their gut bacteria. Mice with balanced gut bacteria were less anxious and aggressive. Researchers at the University of California, Los Angeles (UCLA) tried

out another experiment with two groups of women. The first group was given a milk beverage containing probiotics and the second group was given the same beverage without probiotics. Women who consumed the probiotics were found to have less emotional reactions to external stimuli. A study at the Arizona State University found that kids with autism had a far less diverse microbiome than children without autism.
- Colon cancer: Medical research is now telling us that people who have colon cancer have a different composition of gut microbiota. In fact, they seem to have elevated levels of disease-causing bacteria.
- Arthritis: Individuals suffering from rheumatoid arthritis may possibly have greater volumes of inflammation-linked bacteria than people who do not suffer from the disease.
- Low immunity: Do you always seem to fall ill? Are you the sort of person who can get a cold from a person who sneezed several feet away from you? You are probably suffering from low immunity. If bad bacteria overpowers the good bacteria in your gut, your immunity will indeed decline.
- Leaky gut: According to ayurvedic medicine, most diseases arise from the production of 'ama', a toxic by-product of poor digestion. The *Charaka Samhita* says, 'Due to the purification of the body, the capacity of digestion and metabolism is enhanced, normal health is restored, all sense organs start working with vigour, old age is prevented and diseases cured.' Corelated to this

ayurvedic notion is the idea of 'intestinal permeability'—the leaky gut. The leaky gut is nothing but an inflammation in the digestive tract owing to attacks on the mucosal lining. Eventually, tiny perforations allow larger-than-usual molecules to pass through and poison the bloodstream. Leaky gut can also manifest as skin ailments such as eczema or psoriasis.

What can you do to manage your gut better?

There are several things that you can do to manage your gut better. These include:

- Eat a nutritious diet that is high in fibre-rich foods: These include fruits, vegetables and whole grains. A high-fat, high-sugar, low-fibre diet is the primary suspect in killing some specific types of bacteria thus leaving your microbiota less diverse.
- Take preventive actions and natural remedies instead of using antibiotics: Antibiotics can almost entirely exterminate healthy bacteria while killing bad bacteria. Use antibiotics only when recommended for emergencies by your doctor.
- Use probiotics: Probiotics are beneficial, living bacteria. Consuming probiotic-rich foods and adding a daily natural probiotic supplement are two key strategies that can increase good bacteria in the gut. Remember though that you can't simply consume probiotics to stave off disease. It has to be part of an overall effort.
- Exercise: Surprisingly, exercise also encourages the

growth of several types of gut bacteria. This leads to a more varied microbiota which, in turn, reduces your risk of disease.

- Ensure timely bowel movements: There is no clear rule regarding frequency of bowel movements. Some people evacuate their bowels three times per week while others do it three times a day. Each gut has a specific pattern. It usually takes twenty-four to seventy-two hours for food to travel through your digestive tract. Food does not reach your large intestine—your colon—for at least six to eight hours after eating. So there is no point sitting on the toilet bowl and giving yourself haemorrhoids. But if your schedule is off, you need to review your water intake as well as your intake of fruits and vegetables. If that doesn't solve the problem, you may need a natural laxative. Remember one thing: if you're not having regular motions, your body could be retaining food that you ate days ago. Waste being retained in your gut implies putrefaction inside your body. This can be a serious cause of many other problems.
- Avoid processed foods: Processed foods often lead to inflammation in the lining of our gastrointestinal tract, the very place where food is absorbed by the body. Sometimes, your gut does not identify the processed foods you've eaten as digestible food. Instead, the gut misidentifies ingredients like high-fructose corn syrup or chemical and artificial ingredients as 'invaders'. This results in an inflammatory response—the body is virtually fighting these foods as though they are

infections. Sticking to more whole and unprocessed foods is a simple way to lower gut inflammation.

- Lower gluten intake: Gluten is the general name for the proteins found in wheat, rye and barley. Gluten helps foods maintain their shape—almost like a glue holding the food together. Unfortunately, there's some evidence to show that gluten increases intestinal permeability—what is commonly called a 'leaky gut'. This effectively implies that particles like undigested food and waste, as well as pathogens like bacteria, can cross through the leaky lining of your intestines and get into your bloodstream. This can eventually accelerate inflammation and illness. The ideal way to check if gluten is causing problems for you is to remove gluten completely from your diet for a month and observe what your gut tells you when you reintroduce gluten. Remember to always check labels and ingredient lists. Gluten can often be found in many seemingly-innocent foods such as salad dressing, chewing gum and potato chips. Remember one thing though: eliminating gluten over extended periods tends to reduce the enzymes that our bodies produce to deal with glutens. This can be a problem when glutens are reintroduced to the diet.
- Use prebiotics: Prebiotics work differently from probiotics. Prebiotics are nutrients for the good bacteria in your gut. Examples of prebiotics are onions, legumes, garlic, bananas and asparagus. Prebiotics help nourish your microbiome and balance any negative changes in an altered gut flora caused by antibiotics or even birth

control pills. Antibiotics are ruthless in wiping out all bacteria—even lactobacillus and bifidobacterium that are actually probiotics.

- Consume fermented foods: Fermented foods and beverages such as miso, kimchi, tempeh, yoghurt, sauerkraut, kefir and kombucha contain live cultures. These actually assist your gut to break down and absorb nutrition from your food in addition to enhancing your immunity. If you do not already have fermented foods in your diet, do not jump in with large quantities. Your body may be unable to handle it. Start with smaller portions and work your way up.
- Sleep: Scientists are still trying to figure out whether an improved gut flora can help you sleep better but the reverse is already known—that better sleep improves the bacterial composition in your gut. Getting adequate levels of sleep lowers the level of cortisol and allows enough time for the gut to repair.
- Eat slowly: Eating slowly by chewing your food stimulates production of saliva and sends a signal to your digestive system to get to work. Make it a point to eat slowly and deliberately without distractions such as the phone or television. In India, an oft repeated ayurveda tip by our grandparents is to sit down to eat because standing, walking or driving while eating can inhibit digestion.
- Relax: The more relaxed you are, the better you'll be able to nourish your body — and we're not just talking about digestion. Stress can change your gut, turning it into a

butterfly cage of discomfort. Research shows that taking out some time to meditate can help ease symptoms of gut disorders. For an extra mindful boost, learn which specific probiotic strain is right for your mood.
- Cure leaky gut: As we have seen, a leaky gut results in toxins being released into the bloodstream. Some of the foods that can cure a leaky gut are coconut oil, flax seeds, bone broth, kefir, fermented yoghurt, salmon, steamed vegetables such as broccoli, cauliflower, celery, carrots, cabbage and squash.

When it comes to your gut, no news is good news. If you are hearing no sounds from your gut, are having regular bowel movements and are experiencing no bloating or abdominal pains, you're doing well.

Key Takeaways

- For good health, we only need 80 per cent of our gut bacteria to be good. The remaining 20 per cent can be bad.

- Wrong balance of gut bacteria can cause many problems including inflammatory or irritable bowel, Crohn's disease, obesity, type-2 diabetes, heart disease, anxiety, depression, autism, colon cancer, arthritis, low immunity and leaky gut.

- You can do many things to improve the bacterial balance of your gut. These include eating more fibre, avoiding antibiotics, ensuring timely bowel movements, exercising, avoiding processed foods, reducing gluten intake, using probiotics and prebiotics, adding fermented foods to your diet, eating slowly, getting adequate sleep, meditating and curing a leaky gut.

STEP SIX: ALKALISE

What is more conducive to the breeding of mosquitos—a dirty swamp or a strong flowing river? We know that the dirty swamp is a more fertile ground for mosquitos. The same principle applies to the human body. Our bodies have what is known as an 'internal biological terrain'. When this is balanced, germs associated with illness cannot thrive. When our terrain has a balanced pH we can avoid certain types of cancer, bone and joint deterioration, nervous ailments and digestive troubles.

Mildly acidic compounds are needed within our bodies to keep tissues firm and supple. But if the acidity is overdone, we would have rigid and dry tissues, hardened arteries, hypertension, gout, arthritis, stiffness, pain, anxiety, tension, osteoporosis, kidney stones, insomnia and elevated odds of cancer and infection. On the other hand, a mildly alkaline state creates fluidity, flexibility and relaxation in the body. If alkalinity is overdone, though, we could experience nausea, tissue deterioration, hallucinations, lethargy and mental instability. The solution thus is to maintain a balanced pH.

What is pH? Well, the term 'pH' is an abbreviation for the 'potential of hydrogen' or the concentration of hydrogen ions in a given solution. The pH value indicates the acidity or alkalinity of an element. The pH scale runs from 1 to 14 with 1 being entirely acidic and 14 being entirely alkaline. Water has a neutral pH of 7. Anything below 7 is considered acidic and anything above 7 is considered alkaline.

What is an ideal pH level?

What should the ideal pH level of your body be? As we know, a pH of 7 is neutral. This means that it is as acidic as it is alkaline. But pH levels vary across different parts of your body. In effect, pH depends on where you measure it. Blood serum as well as most body tissues are around 7.365. Saliva and urine are usually on the acidic side lying between 6.4 and 6.8 in a healthy human. The stomach is usually at a pH of around 2. This acidic nature allows the stomach to break down foods properly for digestion.

Most of us do not really think about the acid-alkaline balance of our blood, but a balanced pH is absolutely vital to good health. Increasingly, medical research is telling us that it is better to reduce acidity and increase alkalinity. Consuming an alkaline diet can actually prevent unhealthy microbes from multiplying, tissues from deterioration and organs from damage, essential minerals from being reduced, and the body's immune system from being weakened.

A build-up in the acidic content of your body causes your blood to become acidic. Your kidneys are responsible for maintaining equilibrium in pH and electrolyte levels but owing to the higher acidity in blood, they use vital calcium, magnesium, potassium and sodium to fight the acidity. Effectively, we rob vital minerals from our cells, tissues, organs and bones. Cells become mineral-deficient and are unable to effectively remove waste or oxygenate. Vitamin absorption too is reduced. This is followed by a build-up of toxins and pathogens. You end up compelling your body to work doubly hard to maintain a neutral pH level but this is accomplished by sucking up vital nutrients. Soon, the kidneys begin excreting more minerals via urine. Although you may not have an imbalance in pH, your body will be fatigued and stressed by lower kidney function.

Causes of acidic imbalance

There are many factors that contribute to a build-up of acid in your body. Some of the key ones are:

- Alcohol dependence
- Kidney disease or malfunction
- Use of drugs—including acetazolamide, opioids, sedatives and aspirin
- Overuse of antibiotics
- Bad digestion
- Poor gut health
- Higher consumption of processed and refined foods
- Inadequate intake of potassium, calcium and other minerals
- Low consumption of fibre in diet
- Sedentary lifestyle or inadequate exercise
- Overuse of artificial sweeteners, colouring and preservatives

- Excessive exercise
- Air and water pollution
- Elevated stress levels
- Insomnia or sleep apnea
- Eating too fast
- Pesticides and herbicides in non-organic foods
- Excessive meat consumption
- Added sugar, high sodium, refined grains
- Lower nutrient levels in non-organic food
- Higher hormones in processed foods
- Exposure to chemicals and radiation
- Lung disease, emphysema, chronic bronchitis, pneumonia, pulmonary edema and asthma

What are the benefits of a balanced pH?

Humans today have a diet that is deficient in magnesium, potassium and fibre. In fact, in developed countries, diets tend to be rich in saturated fat, simple sugars, sodium and chloride. Such diets create metabolic acidosis that pulls our bodies away from acid neutrality. What is the solution? Consuming nutrient-dense and alkalising plant foods in parallel to reducing intake of processed foods can be the key solution. A balanced pH level can greatly help in:

- Reducing internal inflammation
- Protecting your body from heart disease
- Lowering the possibility of diabetes
- Preventing formation of kidney stones
- Ensuring stronger bone density

- Preventing calcium build-up in your urine
- Preventing kidney disease or damage
- Enhancing bone mineral density
- Reducing muscle wasting or spasms
- Protecting from vitamin D deficiency
- Relieving lower back pain

Acidosis and types

Acidosis is simply an over-production of acid in the blood or an excessive loss of bicarbonate from the blood. There are five categories of metabolic acidosis which simply means that your body has a poor pH balance or is having to work overtime to maintain a balanced pH.

- Diabetic ketoacidosis: When the liver produces dangerously high amounts of ketone bodies owing to high sugar.
- Hyperchloremic acidosis: When diarrhoea or vomiting causes your body to lose sodium bicarbonate which neutralises your blood.
- Lactic acidosis: Alcoholism, over-exercise, heart failure, liver failure, cancer, seizures, oxygen deprivation or low blood sugar that leads to build up of lactic acid.
- Renal tubular acidosis: This happens when your kidneys are unable to flush out acids to your urine. This leads to acid build-up in your bloodstream.
- Dietary acidosis: This is the result of eating an overly acidic diet that creates unnecessary strain on your body.

How can you work towards a neutral pH level?

Some of the steps that you can take to push your body towards a better acid-alkaline balance are:

- Lower your intake of acidic foods: Some of the foods to reduce in your diet would include processed meats, high-sodium foods, foods that contain added sugar, milk and dairy products, peanuts, refined grains (including white bread, white rice, pasta or breakfast cereals), caffeine, alcohol, fried food, processed cereal grains (examples are corn, wheat, barley, sorghum, millet, rye) and conventional meats (including beef, chicken and pork). Yes, there are some foods that provide excellent nutrition but tend to be higher in acidic content. You would need to eat these in moderation, for example, eggs, lentils, legumes, oats, brown rice, whole grain or sprouted bread and walnuts. Some foods are acidic or alkaline in nature but produce an opposite effect. For example, lemons are highly acidic but they produce an alkalising effect within the body. Alternatively, meat is alkaline but it produces acid in the body.
- Consume an alkaline diet: Include lots of greens in your diet. Remember also that crops grown organically are more alkalising than those that aren't, so buy organic whenever possible. Some of the food items worth adding in your diet are leafy green veggies such as spinach, kale, beet greens and wheat grass; non-starch vegetables such as mushrooms, cucumber, tomatoes, avocado, broccoli, green beans, radish, zucchini, asparagus and cabbage;

healthy fats such as virgin olive oil, coconut oil, nuts, seeds and organic butter; fruits such as grapefruit, citrus fruits and dates; raw or lightly steamed vegetables; starches such as sweet potato, turnips and beets; beans such as navy beans and lima beans; vegetable juices that contain chlorphyll; in addition, you may consider superfoods such as spirulina, apple cider vinegar, seaweed, oregano, garlic and ginger. Supplements that contain alkalising minerals such as potassium and magnesium can also be very helpful.

- Hydrate with alkaline water: There is a great deal of variation in the pH levels of drinking water. When water has a pH value of less than 6.5, it is considered acidic. The ideal way to neutralise the problem is to use pH drops or baking soda. Distilled water is neither acidic nor alkaline with a pH level of 7. Water that is subjected to reverse osmosis (RO) tends to have a pH lower than 7 and is thus slightly acidic. While distilled water and filtered water do not give you the advantage of alkalinity, they are a far better option than tap water or bottled water which are definitely more acidic. Nowadays you can also buy alkaliser bottles that you simply fill up with ordinary water. Just twenty minutes in the bottle gives the water an alkaline pH.
- Lower your dependence on drugs and toxins: Various medicines, chemicals, toxins and pollutants can upset the pH balance of your body. Alcohol, caffeine, opioids, acetazolamide, sedatives, aspirin, carbonic anhydrase inhibitors and non-steroidal anti-inflammatory drugs

are examples of acidity spikers. Work with your doctor to identify the root cause of certain health conditions that may be forcing you to depend on such drugs. It is important to figure out what steps you can take to lower your dependence on such medications.

- Oxygenate: It requires oxygen to burn the nutrients we consume. When there is inadequate oxygen in your blood, this burning capacity is lowered and the net result is acid waste. Deep breathing is a great way to increase oxygen and thus help alkalise the body. Supplements such as liquid chlorophyll can also assist in increasing the oxygen-carrying capacity of blood.
- Improve your digestion: Any food that we do not digest properly creates acid waste. You could be eating the most nutritious high-quality foods but you could still be overacidic if your digestive system is not working adequately. Adding plant enzyme supplements or protein digestive aids can help stimulate hydrochloric acid in the stomach. Yes, it's counter-intuitive but higher hydrochloric acid in your stomach means better digestion and this, in turn, means more alkalinity.
- Lower stress: Our nervous system is made up of two branches: the sympathetic and the parasympathetic. The sympathetic nervous system activates more acid in our bodies when we are under stress. This is in contrast to the parasympathetic system which works to relax us through alkalinity. Meditation, music, deep breathing, yoga and natural stress buster supplements are good options.

- Granny knows best: A couple of home remedies mentioned by Indian grandmothers are worth keeping in mind. One of them is what is called oil-pulling. Take one tablespoon of cold-pressed, unrefined coconut oil and swish it in your mouth for ten minutes and spit out. Older Indians know that this helps maintain a better acid-alkaline balance. Another miracle cure is turmeric.

How can you test your pH level?

You can test your pH using testing strips that are available in pharmacies. You can check your pH with your saliva or urine. Ideally, the second urination of the morning will give you the most accurate results. If testing during the day, one hour before a meal or two hours after a meal are ideal time slots. You will need to compare the resultant colour on the test strip with a colour key that comes in the package. If your body's pH values are in balance, your saliva should average between 6.0 and 7.0 (with 6.4 to 6.6 being the optimal). The pH of your urine should be around 5.0 to 7.5 (with 6.4 to 6.6 being optimal).

KEY TAKEAWAYS

- Mildly acidic compounds are needed within our bodies to keep tissues firm and supple. Alkalinity is needed for fluidity, flexibility and relaxation in the body. Ideally, we need a balance between acidity and alkalinity.

- There are many possible reasons for acid build up. These include alcohol dependence, drug use, overuse of antibiotics, poor digestion or gut health, low fibre consumption, excessive meat consumption, etc.

- Balanced pH has several benefits for the human body. These include reduced internal inflammation, greater protection from heart disease, lower diabetes risk and stronger bone density.

- There are several things you can do to achieve a balanced pH. These include lowering intake of acidic foods, consuming an alkaline diet, drinking alkaline water, lowering your medicine intake under medical supervision, managing stress and better digestion.

STEP SEVEN: BREATHE

Breathing. It's among the most vital physical functions that the human body executes. In fact, every human does it around 20,000 times a day. And still most seem to get it wrong. According to Andrew Weil, a frontrunner in integrative medicine, 'If I had to limit my advice on healthier living to just one tip, it would be to learn to breathe correctly.' Chinese and Indian yogic schools have always emphasised the vital role of 'chi' or 'prana', the life-giving energy that is derived through breath. Unfortunately, it has taken western medicine centuries to catch up.

We breathe throughout the day, everyday and we do not really think about it. But regular breathing and deep breathing are remarkably different. All our cells need oxygen. Some critical organs like the brain cannot remain oxygen-deprived without serious consequences. Thus, it is common sense that enhancing the supply of oxygen to our bodies should make us healthier. But then, common sense isn't that common.

What is wrong with the way we breathe?

Supplying more oxygen to our cells, simply by altering the manner in which we breathe, can actually promote healing—from rather serious ailments such as asthma, chronic pain, poor digestion, atrial fibrillation, depression, and many stress-linked illnesses. The key insight is to revert to a natural respiration pattern of newborn babies. We come into this world breathing deeply but our breathing pattern changes as we age. Tension and stress force us to breathe in a shallow manner—not breathing into our abdomens but merely into our chests. By the time we're adults, we take fifteen to twenty breaths per minute. That's simply too fast. Ideally around five to seven breaths per minute is optimal.

Rapid and shallow breathing is precisely the root cause of many problems. Shallow breathing triggers a message to the adrenal glands that the body is in fight-or-flight mode. The result is that the adrenal glands shoot stress hormones such as cortisol into the bloodstream. When cortisol levels are increased, our immunity cells slow down. Enter disease.

How should we breathe?

The answer thus lies in breathing deeply into your abdomen—not merely into your chest. Deep breathing must always be deep, relaxed, slow and rhythmic. Deep breathing, by definition, is through the nose, not the mouth. It is important to regulate your breaths—around three to four seconds of inhalation and three to four seconds of exhalation. It's quite simple really:

- Inhale through your nose, allowing your belly to expand while feeling the inhaled air fill your chest counting to five.

- Hold your breath counting to three. Allow the oxygen to nourish your cells with healing energy.
- Exhale completely from a slightly parted mouth counting to five and feel your cells releasing expended energy and waste.

Plan your deep breathing during the day in the way that you would schedule business appointments in your diary. Two ten-minute slots each day are ideal. Deep breathing is simple to perform and can be done anywhere—you could be at your desk, in your bed or on public transport. It may take a few days but you will soon begin to notice positive developments in your physical and mental health.

Breathing exercises

Besides the deep breathing technique described earlier, you can also consider alternative breathing exercises or pranayama that can help you undo your defective breathing patterns. Pranayama is the yogic practice of breath control. It is a Sanskrit word that results from the combination of two words—prana and yama. Prana means life and yama means control. Thus, pranayama is a way to control life-energy and thus attain a healthy body and mind. In fact, Patanjali, the great yogic sage, mentions pranayama in the ancient text *Yoga Sutra* as the perfect way to attain samadhi—the most elevated state of meditative consciousness. Pranayama absorbs energy into your body and expels the waste from your living cells. There are some simple pranayama exercises that you can follow for better health.

- Bhastrika Pranayama, also referred to as Bellows Breath: This is a potent breathing technique. It is a cleansing method to clear your nostrils and sinuses. It is also ideal for energising your body. Simply sit in a lotus position with your back upright. Inhale through your nose allowing your lungs to fill up entirely. Breathe out in similar fashion. Repeat this a few times to prepare yourself for Bellows Breath. Now expel rapid breaths through your nose forcefully. Inhale similarly. Remember that your breath should emerge from your diaphragm, and your stomach must move in tandem with your breath although the rest of your body should be still. Alternate a round of bellow breathing with a round of natural breathing. Bhastrika Pranayama done regularly can fortify your lungs and keep asthma in check. It can help calm your mind and prevent allergies, common colds and lack of immunity.
- Kapalbhati Pranayama, also referred to as Skull Shining Breath: This is a breathing exercise that is geared towards giving you a dazzling intellect, hence the term 'skull shining'. Kapalbhati is a means to flush out toxic air from your body. Sit in the usual cross-legged sukhasana position and place your palms on your knees. Entirely focus your attention on your belly. Inhale deeply, calmly and consciously through your nose allowing your lungs to fill up. Pull your stomach in and place your hand on your navel as you breathe in. Then exhale in short, strong and rapid bursts with a hissing sound. Go through a round of Kapalbhati, inhaling and exhaling twenty

times, followed by natural deep breathing. Kapalbhati is said to improve your liver and kidneys while eliminating gas and acidity. It also improves your memory and concentration while rejuvenating your body.

- Bhramari Pranayama, also called Bee Breath (it is named after an Indian species of bee called the bhramari): It is an exceptionally simple method that can be used as a quick-fix to destress. The exhalation is like the buzzing of a bee. Simply sit straight in a position that's comfortable, close your eyes and place your index fingers on the cartilage between your cheeks and ears. Inhale deeply through your nose. Exhale while pressing the cartilage with your index fingers and make a humming sound. Bhramari Pranayama can reduce hypertension, anger, anxiety and migraines.
- Anulom Vilom, also called Alternate Nostril Breathing: Anulom Vilom is a method of balancing your energy. Sit in a comfortable position with your back straight and your chin slightly tucked in towards your chest. Lift your right hand and place your right thumb on the side of your right nostril, blocking it. Inhale deeply and purposefully through your left nostril. After you're done inhaling, press the little finger of your right hand on the side of your left nostril, blocking it while releasing your thumb from the right nostril. Now exhale through your right nostril slowly. Follow that by breathing in through your right nostril, blocking it with your thumb and exhaling through your left nostril. That's one full cycle of Anulom Vilom. Go through five cycles initially, and then increase

it as per convenience. Anulom Vilom done properly can streamline your metabolism, control diabetes, reduce allergies and asthama, and reduce arthritis and sinusitis.
- Bahya Pranayama, also called the External Breath: This is a technique of keeping breath out. Sit straight and inhale deeply. Then exhale completely. Hold your breath, pull your stomach up and bend your neck to gently touch your chest with your chin. Count to five or ten, then inhale deeply and release your chin and stomach. Repeat. Bahya Pranayama provides relief in cases of acidity, diabetes and prostate issues as also urinary and reproductive problems. It also helps fight constipation and gastric problems.

What are the benefits of deep breathing?

- Improves quality of blood: Every cell in the human body needs oxygen. It is a key component in essential cellular activities—the very processes which support life. Simple deep breathing and pranayama not only ensure this but also significantly enhance the quality of your blood.
- Calms you down: 'Just take a deep breath and calm down', is a piece of advice that we have all heard in our lives. It's indeed appropriate. Breathing deeply and slowly permits your nerves to ease. And the increased oxygen to your spinal cord, nerves and the brain enhances the release of pleasure neuro-chemicals, thus putting you in a better mood. Indian yogis knew that there was an intimate relationship between one's breath and one's mind. They

knew that when the mind is agitated, breathing almost certainly gets disturbed. Since yogis were attempting to control the mind, they figured that controlling the breath could possibly regulate the mind. Hence, deep breathing is the first step in meditation.

- Relaxes the muscles: When the nerves are calmed down, the muscles naturally follow. Deep breathing, especially during or after a stressful day at work, can reduce the occurrence of muscle stiffness and can enhance your overall sense of well-being. Deep breathing has been shown to improve stamina too.
- Helps clean out the lungs: We live in a hazardous environment plagued by pollution, smoking habits and poor indoor and outdoor air quality. Lung problems are usually due to particles within the lungs that cause irritation to sensitive tissues. Deep breathing forces oxygen into the deepest parts of your lungs and sweeps out any residue there. Deep breathing also improves lung capacity and performance. Deep breathing exercises are also able to enhance lung function.
- Deep breathing slows your heart rate: Deep breathing strengthens your lungs, thus making them more efficient. This leads to increased oxygen in the blood. By forcing more oxygen into your cells, your heart rate is automatically lowered. The net result is more energy and a less taxed heart.
- Makes the heart stronger: Deep breathing leads to an increased pressure differential in the lungs. This leads to enhanced circulation, thus providing the heart

with respite. A study of thirty-six participants found that thirty days of deep breathing exercises resulted in beneficial changes in heart rate variability which is usually considered an indicator of cardiac autonomic control.

- Releases toxins: Our bodies are designed to expel 70 per cent of our toxins through breathing. Poor breathing means that you are inadequately expelling toxins. When you exhale you release carbon dioxide—metabolic waste—that has been transferred from your bloodstream into your lungs.
- Decreases blood pressure: Deep breathing relaxes your muscles as well as the arteries and veins—the pipes that carry our blood. The result of that relaxation is a lowered blood pressure.
- Vital in management of psychological issues: In 2005, medical researchers Richard Brown and Patricia Gerbarg found that that breathing deeply and frequently has a positive effect on depression and other anxiety-related disorders. Deep breathing has been shown to improve the symptoms of Obsessive-compulsive disorder (OCD) and Post-traumatic Stress Disorder (PTSD).
- Improves sleep: Those who suffer from depression are aware of the side effect—poor sleep quality. A study that observed the effects of deep breathing therapy over a month found that their quality of sleep improved considerably.
- Internal organ massage: Your diaphragm movement during deep breathing exercises results in a gentle

internal massage of the stomach, small intestine, liver, pancreas and even heart. This massaging action improves circulation within them. Deep breathing also strengthens your abdominal muscles.
- Strengthens immunity: Oxygen is transported through your bloodstream by attachment to haemoglobin in your red blood cells, thus prompting your body to metabolise nutrients and vitamins that improve immunity.
- Relieves pain: Have you considered what happens to your breath when you anticipate pain? You may have shortened breath or you may hold your breath. There is an intimate connection there. Breathing can help ease your pain. Some research studies have found that using deep breathing exercises as a relaxation technique are effective in managing pain for patients who had recently undergone coronary artery bypass graft surgery. 73 per cent of the subjects found that deep-breathing was helpful in managing their pain. Deep and Slow Breathing (DSB) methods were also effective in managing chronic pain.
- Reduces inflammation: A study in 2016 studied participants going through twenty minutes of deep breathing. When their saliva was checked at five-minute intervals, it was found that subjects showed significant changes in the salivary cytokines—these are biomarkers for inflammation. In effect, deep breathing has an effect on our molecular-level physiology almost instantly.
- Weight control: Obesity is a significant problem and many people turn to diets for weight loss. These diets

often result in hunger pangs—or stomach contractions. Those who are fasting or undertaking calorie-restricted diets face problems from such pangs. It has been found that dieters are significantly able to reduce or suppress hunger pangs through deep breathing. If you are overweight, extra oxygen burns your fat better; on the other hand, if you are underweight, extra oxygen feeds your tissues and glands better. Deep breathing also improves glycemic response. Diaphragmatic breathing is also found to be effective in reducing oxidative stress in diabetics.

- Alleviates Irritable Bowel Syndrome: IBS impairs millions of people worldwide and is often connected with stress-related ailments. One study found that deep breathing coupled with yogic asanas could alleviate IBS even better than Loperamide, a standard IBS drug. Deep breathing can even help in the treatment of Gastroesophageal Reflux Disease (GERD).
- Increases digestion and assimilation: When digestive organs such as the stomach receive more oxygen, they operate more effectively. Digestion is further improved by food being oxygenated even more.
- Improves focus and memory: One study found that just ten minutes of deep breathing, six days a week for six weeks, resulted in overall improvement in scores on a rapid-fire arithmetic test and playing card test. Another study found that participants who underwent a half-hour alternate-nostril breathing session had improved memory recall twenty-four hours after the session.

- Increases energy: Deep breathing has been shown to increase growth hormone (GH) and dehydroepiandrosterone sulphate (DHEAS), two key hormones associated with aging. Just twelve weeks of yogic breathing was found to increase GH and DHEAS in both males and females. If you are always feeling tired, deep breathing can assist. Unfortunately, most people don't use their diaphragms to breathe, instead using weaker surrounding muscles. Better breathing results in more oxygen saturation in the cells, thus improving your energy and stamina.
- Improves posture: Good breathing practices over extended periods of time will eventually encourage good posture as good posture and good breathing are intrinsically connected.
- Increases muscle mass: Deep breathing means more oxygenation to all the cells in your body. This increased oxygenation increases muscle mass. In fact, deep breathing is known to correlate with lower levels of cortisol and higher levels of melatonin. Effectively, deep breathing can protect athletes from the adverse effects of exercise-related stress.
- Reduce addictions: Deep breathing can help manage addictions better. One particular study found that yogic breathing exercises were a possible way to help smokers curb nicotine cravings.

Key Takeaways

- Every human takes around 20,000 breaths per day. As babies we breathe deeply but our breathing pattern changes as we age. Tension and stress force us to breathe in a shallower manner that is not good for us.

- Setting aside some time in the day for deep breathing into the abdomen is a healthy practice. Plan your deep breathing during the day in the way that you would schedule business appointments in your diary. Two ten-minute slots each day are ideal.

- There are some simple pranayama exercises such as bhastrika, kapalbhati, bhramari, anulom vilom and bahya pranayam that can help you improve your health through breath.

- There are many benefits of deep breathing. These benefits include calming the mind, relaxing the muscles, cleaning the lungs, lowered heart rate, releasing toxins, lowering blood pressure, improving sleep, strengthening immunity, improving digestion, and enhancing memory.

STEP EIGHT: SUPPLEMENT

Read any magazine or blog and you'll find dozens of recommendations for health supplements that people swear by—turmeric pills, goji berry, maca pills, kale powder, spirulina ... the list is endless. But as a wise man once said, 'Advertisers constantly invent cures for which there is no disease.'

Many of the supplements out there are gimmicks. And frankly, there is simply no substitute for getting vital nutrients from your food. The golden rule is to get your nutrients from whole foods *first* and *then* supplement only if needed. There are simply too many individuals who have terrible eating habits, drink, smoke, and think that they can cure everything by taking a few supplements. This is a fallacy.

Assuming that you eat a well-balanced diet and lead a healthy life, there is still a strong case for supplements that can take care of specific deficiencies that you may be experiencing at any given point in time. For example, folate may be consumed by women who are trying to conceive or even women who are pregnant. Iron and vitamin B12 deficiencies are often found in individuals who follow a vegan or vegetarian diet and appropriate supplements may be in order for such people. Calcium supplements may be required by those who have lactose intolerance because they are unable to get calcium from dairy products. People who work indoors for long hours or bedridden patients may need vitamin D to compensate for lack of exposure to sunlight. Those recovering from a bout of antibiotics may need probiotics to restore the bacterial balance of the gut.

The important thing is that taking supplements should not become a free-for-all. Some supplements have side effects and it is best to take the advice of a doctor before consuming any. Here are a few supplements that you may consider taking (but please take expert medical advice before doing so). You will notice that some of the supplements mentioned in the list below have been recommended by Indian elders, particulary grandmothers, over many generations.

- Fish oil: A vital nutrient is long chain omega-3 fat that is found naturally in oily fish such as salmon. Research shows that omega-3 fatty acids are good for a healthy heart and brain. In fact, they can also lower inflammation in the human body. Fish oil is bursting with omega-3 fatty acids but other options to get your dose of omega-3 include cod liver oil tablets, flaxseeds, flaxseed oil, walnuts and chia seeds.
- Probiotics: These are the beneficial bacteria that line our gut and assist in absorption and fighting infection. Modern research is increasingly telling us that there is a direct link between gut health and our immune

system. Supplementing your daily diet with a probiotic can be an effective solution to keeping your gut healthy. There are different strains of probiotics. While some boost immunity, others assist in digestion or regulating hormonal balance. Some probiotic sources are kombucha, yoghurt, kefir, sauerkraut, miso and tempeh.
- Vitamin D: This is vital for strong bones and muscles. It is a fat-soluble micronutrient that is critically needed by humans for survival. The best source of vitamin D is sunlight. You only require about fifteen to twenty minutes of daily exposure to get your quota. However, for those who spend most of their time indoors, a vitamin D supplement may be a good idea.
- Magnesium: This plays a pivotal role in many enzymatic reactions. These include metabolising food, synthesising fatty acids and proteins and even conveying nerve impulses. Magnesium can also result in better sleep and lower stress levels.
- Bacopa Monnieri: Famously known as brahmi in India, this is an excellent tonic for the brain and nervous system. Brahmi aids in disposing toxins and blockages from the nervous system and helps with depression, memory and concentration. It is also excellent for hair growth.
- Protein: Some individuals can derive benefit from protein supplementation. In particular, this applies to athletes, bodybuilders, vegetarians and vegans. Protein aids weight loss by increasing metabolism and reducing hunger. Vegan protein powder that is made from plant-

based protein is a good option to consider as also whey protein.
- Calcium: About 99 per cent of your body's calcium is in your bones. An appropriate level of calcium intake is good for bone health. While milk, yogurt, green leafy vegetables and cheese are excellent sources of calcium, dietary restrictions may make the required number of servings impossible. A supplement can help fill this gap.
- Carom: Called ajwain in India, this is a strong digestive and nerve stimulant. It also aids weight loss by sucking out toxins from the body. It is also useful in healing painful joints.
- Wintery Cherry: This is called ashwagandha in India. Ashwagandha is considered to be one of the best anti-aging herbs. It can improve body composition, hormones and even fertility. Ashwagandha is an adaptogen, thus improving your stress response and cortisol levels.
- Turmeric: Turmeric or haldi is a blood purifier and liver cleanser. The anti-inflammatory and bioactive compound in turmeric is curcumin that can help with a variety of inflammatory conditions including arthritis.
- Zinc: Zinc supplements are useful in keeping your immune system healthy, promoting good skeletal development and maintaining your energy metabolism at higher levels.
- Cardamom: Cardamom or elaichi is a natural tranquiliser. It is said to bring clarity to mind and also has a mood elevation effect. Cardamom can neutralise the acidic effect of coffee as also the mucus-forming properties in milk.

- Cumin: Cumin or jeera improves the digestive system and metabolism while helping the body with nutrient absorption. Cumin is particularly useful for new mothers because it improves milk secretion.
- Licorice: Called mulethi in India, licorice is a rejuvenating herb that reduces acidity and calms the mind. Mulethi is a storehouse of many essential phytonutrients, including beta-carotene, thymol, phenol and quercetin. Mulethi has expectorant, demulcent, anti-inflammatory, anti-ulcer, laxative, anti-viral, anti-fungal, anti-bacterial, anti-oxidant and anti-tumour properties.
- Rubia Cordifolia: Known to ayurveda as manjistha, this is probably the best blood purifying herb that has significant anti-inflammatory properties. Manjistha detoxifies the blood and liver and can also help clear acne. It also helps regulate liver and kidney functions.
- Azadirachta Indica: Known to millions of Indians as neem, this is a powerful blood purifier and detoxifier. It works amazingly for acne, eczema, psoriasis, other skin diseases, wound healing and skin damage. It is also helpful in easing joint and muscle pain.
- Iron: If you are low and sluggish, you may have an iron deficiency. Iron is responsible for carrying oxygen throughout the body and for the formation of red blood cells.
- Vitamin C: Vitamin C is the most widely used single vitamin because it is not only an anti-oxidant but is also a remedy for the common cold. Some research indicates that it may have cancer preventing properties too.

- Cinnamon: Cinnamon or dalchini is loaded with anti-oxidants and has anti-inflammatory properties. It has also been linked to reduced odds of heart disease. Most importantly, cinnamon improves insulin sensitivity and can lower blood sugar levels.
- Spirulina: Spirulina is an algae that grows in tropical climates. It is a very rich source of anti-oxidants, such as proteins, vitamins, minerals and fatty acids. Spirulina is thus often added to healthy shakes and smoothies for overall health and wellness. It also slows the release of histamine, thus helping those suffering from allergies.
- Glucosamine: Glucosamine is found naturally in the body as a combination of glucose and the amino acid, glutamine. Glucosamine is responsible for cartilage and tissue repair and can alleviate osteoporosis and rheumatoid arthritis. Unfortunately, our natural production slows as we age. Glucosamine supplementation can act as a protective barrier for our joints.
- Basil: Known as tulsi in India, it is regarded as a tonic for the body, mind and spirit. Tulsi is excellent for reducing stress and anxiety. It also improves immunity to fight infections, besides helping lower cholesterol.
- Sesamin: Sesamin is a lignan found in sesame seeds. It is a nutritional supplement that not only provides anti-oxidant and anti-inflammatory effects but also modulates estrogen receptors and fat burning. Sesamin helps oxidise fat cells to help fat burn and also sends signals to the body telling it to store less fat from incoming calories.

Multi-vitamin and Multi-mineral

Many health issues are often linked to a root cause of vitamin or mineral deficiency. Unfortunately, our food loses many nutrients by the time it is harvested, refined, packed, transported and eventually sold via stores. Also, in India, we tend to overcook our food. Overcooking takes away most of the nutritional content from it. Moreover, certain medical conditions like irritable bowel syndrome (IBS) makes absorption of nutrients difficult even if we are eating a balanced diet. In such cases, taking a natural multi-vitamin and a natural multi-mineral supplement can be a good idea because it can keep your body enriched with essential nutrients. However, supplements should be taken under medical supervision, as certain studies suggest that consuming them in excess can cause more harm to your health than good.

The better option therefore is to meet your vitamin and mineral requirements through natural foods. Follow the chart below to know which foods to eat for adequate nutrition.

Vitamin A	Carrots, sweet potatoes, apricots, spinach and kale
Vitamin B3	Mushrooms, avacodos, peanuts, green peas and beets
Vitamin C	Strawberries, tomato, broccoli, cabbage, lemon, lychees and papayas
Vitamin E	Spinach, broccoli, almonds and peanuts

Folic acid supplements are recommended if you're pregnant, or if you want to get pregnant. Also, vitamin D is difficult to get from the foods we eat, but is a critical ingredient, as it keeps your bones strong by helping your body absorb calcium. Getting sunlight helps our bodies produce it, but it can be tough to get enough sunlight, especially in the winters. Vitamin D supplements are therefore recommended but not without consulting a doctor.

> **KEY TAKEAWAYS**
>
> - The golden rule is to get your nutrients from whole foods first and then supplement only if needed.
>
> - Assuming that you eat a well-balanced diet and lead a healthy life, there is still a strong case for supplements that can take care of specific deficiencies that you may be experiencing at any given point in time.
>
> - Taking supplements should not become a free-for-all. Some supplements have side effects and it is best to take the advice of a doctor before taking them.
>
> - Some of the supplements that you may consider: fish oil, probiotics, vitamin D, magnesium, brahmi, protein, calcium, ajwain, ashwagandha, haldi, zinc, elaichi, jeera, mulaithi, manjistha, neem, iron, vitamin C, dalchini, spirulina, glucosamine, tulsi and sesamin.

STEP NINE: LOVE

Love yourself… When someone tells us this, the obvious reaction from most of us is, 'Of course, I love myself. Everyone does that. Isn't that natural?' It might seem natural, but believe me it's not easy for many. In my practice I have seen people, especially teens and young adults, locking themselves up in their own personal prison and punishing themselves for varied reasons—a broken relationship, a job rejection, exam failure and so on. They desperately want to get out of the hole, but can't. They've lost self-confidence and it all started because they stopped loving themselves. Consider the story of Raima:

Raima was a twenty-one-year-old young marketing executive who weighed 89 kilos. With a short frame of just over 5 feet and her weight more than what her body could take, Raima faced a lot of fat-shaming every day. She clearly remembers an incident where once at a crowded mall, she heard someone walking behind her say, 'Malls will definitely get crowded if they let elephants walk inside freely.' It wounded her deeply. Says Raima, 'There were times when I pinched the fat on my belly and thought can someone cut this crap out.' In a desperate attempt to lose her body fat, she joined a gym. With mirrors everywhere at the gym, she used to see herself while working out and every time she saw her obese body, she got depressed. She checked her weight every day and the numbers on her weighing scale hardly showed any different result! She started hating her body and lost her self-confidence.

I am sure many will relate to Raima's story. You, too, will relate to it if you have stopped loving yourself because you felt rejected or disappointed with life. You will relate to it if you have ever felt that you were not competent enough to be in this world or you thought you were ugly, stupid or weird. So what do you do?

Let's see what Raima did to get her life back on track. She just followed a simple piece of advice from her gym instructor who told her, 'Work out because you love your body and not because you hate it! If you work out because you hate your body, you will take exercise as a punishment and how can anyone enjoy punishment? If you don't enjoy it, you won't do it wholeheartedly and will not get the desired results. However, if you love your body, you will feel that you are worth every effort you make to become healthy.' This positive attitude worked wonderfully for Raima and there is no reason why it will not work for you. Today, Raima weighs 60 kilos, feels good, looks great and is being complimented for her new found identity.

Remember Imtiaz Ali's movie *Jab We Met*? Kareena Kapoor uses a particular line that is etched in our memories—*Main apni favourite hoon.* Yes, be your own favourite. It is the perfect technique to keep all your haters at bay and keep negativity out of your life. Gautam Buddha said, 'You can search throughout the entire universe for someone who is more deserving of your love and affection than you are yourself, and that person is not to be found anywhere. You yourself, as much as anybody in the entire universe deserves your love and affection.'

One of my patients once told me, 'A year ago, I almost went into depression after a bad break-up. I had given so much of my energy to make that relationship work that I had completely neglected my own needs and my happiness. When that addictive and painful relationship finally ended, I had to live with the after-effects of a lack of self-love. I had forgotten how to love myself.'

So, what does loving yourself exactly mean?

It is simply the art of self-acceptance. It means to have self-respect and a positive self-image. Loving yourself means understanding that your weight, your hair or skin colour, your style of dressing, or the way you talk or walk does not make you any less attractive than anyone else. Loving yourself means having the courage to forgive yourself and acknowledge the fact that you are a human being and it is just human to make mistakes. Loving yourself means understanding what makes your soul happy, and doing things as frequently as you can to achieve that happiness. It also means realising that not everyone will love you, and that not everybody has to love you, but you can always and forever love yourself and therefore take care of your mental, physical and emotional well-being. This includes eating healthy, getting enough sleep, doing regular exercise, finding time for your hobby and taking good care of your health.

Loving yourself also means investing in your health

People do not think twice before spending money on expensive clothes, gadgets, accessories, cars or vacations but when it comes to spending on their health, they have reservations. Remember that your body will be around a lot longer than that expensive handbag. Your body needs your attention. It is the temple of your self-being. The two excuses I hear as to why people don't take care of their health are because of lack of time or money. We value time and money more because we believe them to be a component of more important things in life like family and work. What people fail to realise is that if you don't have your health, then nothing else matters. You and your family will suffer if your health is not good. People will do 'whatever it takes' to get healthy but only when they are diseased. They do very little to 'invest' in their health. Waiting to be sick and then treating it is like investing in disease. Why not invest in health? The choice is yours: either spend money to buy health now or save it to treat a disease later.

In an attempt to 'do it all' and make others happy, some people literally neglect themselves and their health. Take a look at the women in average Indian homes—mothers or wives. They're busy raising kids, working, caring for elderly parents, running a household … they do it all. They are so busy taking care of everyone else that they aren't taking care of themselves. They forget that they are important too.

I remember the case of a young woman, who a few years ago never stepped out of the house unless she was sure that she looked her best. Today she confidently steps out in her track suit to pick up her son from school. Just because you are a mom doesn't mean you cannot look good. You have every right to look and feel attractive. Women, especially mothers, should remember this and should reinforce this to their husbands and children every single day.

- Take care of your needs too. If your children constantly see you putting your needs on the back burner, they will be more inclined to do the same. Remember that what you do today can determine the kind of life your child will lead tomorrow.
- Eat on time. It is fine sometimes if you have food before your husband or children when they get late. Only if your health is good will you be able to take care of the health of your loved ones.
- Do not eat leftover food just because you do not want to waste it (find other ways how not to waste food). Mothers and wives harm themselves by being the family 'dustbins'.
- Invest in yourself. Go for regular body check-ups.
- Do not ignore the warning signs your body is giving if something is wrong. Take immediate medical help.
- Keep aside some time in a day only for yourself.
- Find ways to connect with friends.

Loving yourself is a great way to achieve good health

Though it is difficult to understand how it could possibly have an effect on your body, believe it or not, it does. Recognising your self-worth, having confidence in your abilities and loving and accepting your body increases the flow of good hormones like endorphins and anti-oxidants in the body. This, in turn, helps with cellular repair, improves the delivery of oxygen, helps to supply nutrients to tissues and helps to eliminate the toxic waste from the body. Consider the story of Shital:

Twenty-eight-year-old Shital suffered from acne for more than three years. She applied several ointments and creams and swallowed many oral medications. Some dermatologists advised hormone replacement therapy that worked temporarily but the acne appeared as soon as she stopped the medicines. She finally decided to resort to homeopathy. While taking her medical and personal history, we found that Shital felt that she was neglected as a child. She felt that her parents gave her siblings more attention and love than what she received. She got married to a person who was dominating and who would only dictate his terms and conditions. She felt that no one really loved her and therefore she stopped taking care of herself. Homeopathy helped Shital to get rid of her low self-esteem and deep-rooted insecurities—and consequently her acne.

Illnesses or symptoms like acne that appear on the body are sometimes manifestations of what goes on inside your body. Stress, insecurities, self-hatred and self-doubt all have an impact on your health. As soon as you rid yourself of these fears and start accepting and loving yourself, these symptoms disappear.

How does loving yourself help?

- It frees you from what is not good for you mentally and physically.
- Negativity or criticism does not affect you.
- You don't regret doing or not doing anything because you believe in your decisions and have faith in your abilities.
- It introduces you to self-confidence you never knew you had. You become independent and stop looking for support from others.
- It helps you cope with stress.

What can you do to love yourself?

- Remind yourself that you are important. Do things for your mental, emotional and spiritual self first so that you can share this goodness with people you love and care for.
- Don't blame yourself for everything that goes wrong. Part of loving yourself is keeping things easy and being kind to yourself. Remember you are a human being and it's only human to make mistakes. So don't blame yourself for everything that goes wrong at home or at work.
- Do one small thing every day that makes you happy. It can be as quick and easy as you like. For example,

if you like to listen to music or your favourite radio jockey, but aren't really finding time for it, take out just ten minutes in a day and tune in to your favourite radio station. These ten minutes should be yours without any distractions. Once you can easily give ten minutes to yourself, attempt to slowly increase it.

- Think positive and be confident. Change is easier when it's based on positive thinking rather than on guilt, shame or fear. So be and think positive. Do whatever it takes to increase your self-confidence and love who you are.
- Create a support system: One great way to feel good is to know that you have a support system. It could be a friend, spouse, coach, family member or whoever you feel comfortable with. Build connections. It really helps when you have someone to share any roadblocks or wins you have along the way.

Beyond loving yourself: Your relationships

There is profound truth in the notion that a meaningful relationship can make one healthier. There are good as well as bad days in our life. While good days are always easier to spend the way we like, when things do not go the way we want them to, we all look out for support and encouragement. For those who try to sort out their tough times alone, it is often a difficult battle to fight. On the other hand, when there is support from family, friends or colleagues, we can deal with these problems more logically. Before we reach a breaking point, we should have a system in place to help us sail safely through those rough seas. Consider the example of Gayatri:

Gayatri was enjoying one of the happiest moments of her life when she gave birth to her first child, a healthy and adorable son. Little did she know that one of the toughest phases of her life was about to begin soon. Just two months after the birth of her baby, she accidently broke her ankle and had to undergo a surgery. The next few months were the most difficult period she had ever gone through in her life. She underwent surgery, agonising pain post-surgery and was unable to walk for the next four months.

Ask Gayatri about her strength in this challenging phase of her life, and she says it's her family, her biggest support system. It was her parents, her in-laws and her husband who made her life much easier in those tough times. She couldn't even imagine what life would have been without their support. She was dependent on them for almost everything, which included helping her even with routine stuff like bathing and wearing clothes. Plus, she had to take care of her baby too. All this wouldn't have been possible if she had no family support. She is glad that she had invested her time and energy in developing this strong support system for years and it was the love that she gave to her family that came back to her in times when it was most required.

There are many health benefits of having a healthy relationship. Before we discuss these benefits, let us understand what healthy relationships are. Can only two partners who are romantically involved have a positive healthy relationship? Not at all. Any two people who love, support, encourage and help each other practically as well as emotionally can share a positive relationship. It has been seen that people with good quality friendships handle stress much better.

Research indicates that affection between parents, children and close friends can help the brain, heart and other body systems. Lionel Kauffman once quipped, 'Children are a great comfort in your old age. And they help you reach it faster, too.' Yes, family equations are always tricky. But one simply cannot sufficiently emphasise the value of those relationships.

So, what are the signs of a healthy relationship? People in healthy relationships tend to:

- Listen to each other
- Communicate without being judgmental
- Trust as well as respect each other
- Make time for each other and value each other's time
- Engage in healthy activities together

Twenty-five-year old Sunny Pawar spent four years of his life struggling to keep his paralysed girlfriend Aarti alive and in good health. Aarti, who had a car accident in 2006, could not even recognise Sunny. The injury she sustained had taken away her ability to communicate. Sunny, who was in a relationship with her since fifteen months before the accident, gave up his education to take care of her. He spent twelve hours a day by her side. His story of courage and endurance was covered in many leading newspapers in 2007. After struggling with life for four years, Aarti passed away at the age of twenty-three. Sunny lost his love but he definitely found a way to rise above his struggles. Just after Aarti passed away, in one of his interviews, Sunny mentioned, 'I am drawing strength from the fact that she lived for so long after the accident, when doctors had given up all the hope of her surviving even for a few months. This, I believe, is the power of our love and the healthy bond we shared. Said Aarti's mother, 'With them, I realised how much a support in the form of love can encourage and give strength to people even in the most hopeless situations in life.' Sunny admits that both he and Aarti had worked on developing a strong relationship. He had learned from Aarti that if you believed in something, be prepared to go all the way, right up to the finish line. That's exactly what he did!

Beneficial romantic relationships

While it is not necessary that you have to be romantically involved to enjoy the benefits of a healthy relationship, a healthy romantic relationship can have a positive impact on your health.

- Less stress: Being in a committed relationship is linked to lower production of cortisol, a stress hormone.
- Better healing power: I have seen that people who are in a healthy committed relationship or are happily married have better chances of healing post medical treatment or surgery. Whether it is having someone there to remind you to take medicines on time, or having a partner to help take your mind off the pain, married people have better chances of healing. There are studies that indicate

that happily married patients who have undergone heart surgery are three times more likely to survive the first three months after surgery than single patients. Married patients also feel more confident about their ability to handle post-surgery pain. A little emotional support can go a long way toward helping a person recover from a procedure or illness.

- Healthier habits: A healthy relationship can set the perfect tone for a healthy lifestyle. If your spouse, friend or other loved ones encourage eating a healthy diet, exercising, not smoking and other healthy habits, you are likely to follow their footsteps. It is a lot easier to take on healthy habits when you surround yourself with people who are doing the same.
- Less pain: A study indicates that when people are 'deeply in love' and look at a photo of their partner, they actually feel less pain than those who don't have anyone to look at romantically. Researchers found that the dopamine system that is deployed when you are in love can create its own form of natural painkillers, lessening the severity of pain.
- Add more years to life: Speaking of adding years onto your life, there are studies that indicate that having healthy relationships makes a bigger impact on avoiding early death. One study even suggests that a lack of social relationships has the same effect on health as smoking fifteen cigarettes a day.
- Healthy intimacy: Sex and physical intimacy are a part of life. Some of the benefits you can get from sex include

lower blood pressure, calorie burn, deeper sleep, better heart health and a stronger immune system. In a study of immunity in people in romantic relationships, people who had frequent sex (one to two times a week) had more immunoglobulin A (IgA) in their saliva—this is the antibody that plays a role in preventing illnesses.

Pet relationships

Not only human beings but even animals can give us happiness. When we come home to a pet at the end of a stressful day, we feel a sudden wave of calmness within us. This isn't just our imagination but it has been scientifically proven that pets do a lot of good to our physical and mental health, as they often provide unconditional acceptance. And, it's not only about love and affection; owning a pet can also decrease depression, stress and anxiety. It can lower our blood pressure, improve immunity and even decrease risk of heart attack and stroke, not to mention the extra exercise we get from walks and playing with them. Considering the health benefits of bonding with pets, dogs are now trained to become therapy dogs that provide affection, comfort and love to people in hospitals, retirement homes, nursing homes and schools, and to people with anxiety disorders or autism.

How can you develop a healthy relationship?

Here are ten things you can do to make your relationship strong and healthy.

- Have an open and honest communication channel: One of the most important components for a healthy positive relationship is an open and honest communication channel. Do not expect your partner to read your mind, and don't try to read his or her mind either. Instead, ask honest questions and give honest answers. Honesty is still the best policy to make any relationship strong. Work to create an environment in which each of you can feel safe expressing thoughts, feelings, hopes and dreams with the other.
- Be empathetic: This is the ability to understand and express interest in other person's feelings and point of view. No, it doesn't mean that you have to agree with everything he or she has to say. Just acknowledge it and try to understand.
- Acceptance: Understand that you can't make your friend or partner change. If you really value your relationships, take responsibility for your own feelings, attitudes and actions rather than trying to change the other person.
- Value others and be a good listener: Know that people want to be valued and appreciated. Also, be a good listener. Maintain good eye contact when the other person is talking and listen before you give your opinion.
- Show appreciation often: Simple words like 'thank you' even for little things show that you are not taking each other for granted. Spontaneous hugs and kisses are reminders that you love and value your partner.

- Provide emotional and physical support: Support each other emotionally and in practical ways. Divide up the day-to-day workload in a way that makes each of you comfortable.
- Give time: Time is the most valuable gift you can give people whom you value. Giving people time is like giving a portion of your life that you will never get back.
- Make yourself available: Support others when they need it and make yourself available at critical times. There is a beautiful saying, 'Respect people who find time for you in their busy schedule, but love people who never look at their schedule when you need them.'
- Laugh often: Laugh with your friends each day, either in person or on the phone.
- Keep the playfulness alive: If you are involved in a romantic relationship, have fun together; do fun activities together even if it means doing some stupid things, and keep the physical intimacy alive. Remember, it is an important part of your relationship.

Key Takeaways

- Love must start with self-love, which is the art of self-acceptance. It means having self-respect and a positive self-image. Loving yourself also means investing in your own health.

- You can do several things to love yourself—remind yourself that you are important, stop blaming yourself for things that go wrong, do one thing each day that makes you happy, think positive and create a support system.

- Any two people who love, support, encourage and help each other practically as well as emotionally can share a positive relationship that makes it easier to handle the stresses and pressures of life.

- Beneficial romantic relationships can lower stress, improve your body's healing power, add years to your life, encourage healthier habits and promote healthy intimacy.

- It has been shown that keeping a pet can have significant health benefits too.

- Some of the things that you can do to maintain a healthy relationship are honest and open communication, empathy, acceptance, being a good listener, showing appreciation, providing emotional support, laughing together and keeping the playfulness alive.

STEP TEN: PREVENT

The philosopher Lao-Tzu said, 'Anticipate the difficult by managing the easy.' And you know what? It is actually quite easy to do. The human body is engineered in such a miraculous way that it usually sends some warning signs to indicate that something is wrong. However, in the chaos of everyday life, we tend to dismiss these signals like a morning alarm. Sometimes we even fail to recognise certain changes that manifest in our bodies. Even if we recognise these signals, we try to fix them with some sort of medication or quick relief formula, without even thinking about the root cause of the problem.

Cartoonist Caryn Leschen correctly observed, 'Thirty-five is when you finally get your head together and your body starts falling apart.' Do not ignore signs that your body sends out as warning signals of something not right within. These problems most often do not occur overnight but are built up over time, making them difficult to notice.

Twenty-five-year-old Gauri was suffering from excessive hair fall. The volume of her hair had reduced to half the original. She visited her family physician who suggested some iron supplements and recommended a hair oil to control hair loss. However, her hair continued to fall. She later visited our trichologist who studied her case, even probing her personal life. Gauri was in a steady relationship but was worried that her parents would not agree to this inter-faith marriage. It emerged that stress was resulting in insufficient sleep. She was counselled and treated for stress. As her sleep returned, so did her hair. So if you, too, are suffering from hair loss, remember that one of the reasons might be stress, or lack of sleep.

Consider yet another case:

Thirty-year-old Malti was experiencing frequent episodes of sudden increase in her heart rate, spikes and dips in blood pressure, dizziness and shortness of breath. It all started while she was relaxing at home one night. For a few minutes, she thought she was going to die. In parallel, her skin had become dry and flaky. She went in for a medical consultation and was diagnosed with a serious heart ailment. The doctor prescribed strong medications usually recommended for a heart disorder. These only made her condition worse. She was unable to exercise because she felt fatigued and ran out of breath very quickly. She began to gain weight which only magnified the problem. She decided to take a second opinion and Malti came to me. I found out that she had an extremely stressful work life and consumed a great deal of coffee in order to meet work commitments. Her high caffeine consumption was causing dehydration that was resulting in increased heart rate, varying blood pressure and dry and flaky skin. We asked her to reduce her caffeine intake and increase her intake of water. Slowly and steadily her condition improved and she started to run. Running helped her avoid triggers like caffeine. She is now physically fit and her heart beat, blood pressure and weight are normal. In fact, she recently ran a marathon.

Think about it. Did you ever imagine that something as simple as consuming coffee or worrying about a relationship could impact your health so significantly? Your body sends out a lot of signals indicating that there is something wrong with what you are doing to it. It could be lifestyle issues like heavy intake of caffeine, alcohol, too much stress, wrong eating, inadequate sleep and even excess physical activity. So, pay attention to your body—your hair, skin, teeth, nails, waistline and the other parts and functions of your body. They all give signals if something goes wrong and needs to be fixed. The following tips will help you identify these signals and take appropriate action.

- Hair: Dry and thin hair, which is prone to breakage, may be a precursor for hypothyroidism. Sometimes, our hair gets too dry and lacks lustre, standing out like thin straw. This dry, brittle hair that breaks easily may also be a sign of iron-deficiency anaemia. It affects nearly 60 per cent of Indian women. Hair loss in small, circular patches can be a sign of autoimmune disorders (for example, systemic lupus erythromatosis, or SLE), early-onset diabetes and thyroid disease. A scaly scalp may be due to psoriasis, a skin disorder. Hair loss can also indicate that you are stressed. This manifests itself in seborrheic dermatitis, a chronic skin condition with dandruff-like large scales and excessive oilyness of the scalp.

- Skin: An itchy skin and the delayed healing of wounds can be an indication of diabetes. A dull skin with brittle nails might indicate thyroid problems. Excessive sweating can indicate an overactive thyroid. A dry and scaly skin might indicate skin ailments like psoriasis or eczema. Excessive itchiness may also be a signal your body is trying to give you when you are suffering from liver disease.
- Oral health: Inflamed or bleeding gums can be a sign of diabetes or can also indicate low intake of vitamin C. Loss of teeth, mouth ulcers and dental caries are signs of a poor diet. Overconsumption of soft drinks is significantly associated with dental caries.
- Weight gain or loss: Unintentional weight gain or loss can be an indication of PCOD or thyroid. In women, an irregular menstrual cycle can also indicate PCOD. While being overweight is one of the body's signal of poor health, apple-shaped individuals (who carry extra weight around the waist and belly) are at higher risk of heart disease.
- Urine colour: Keeping yourself well-hydrated is essential for maintaining a healthy body. Your urine is almost completely clear when you are well-hydrated. However, if you see dark yellow-coloured urine, you are probably not drinking enough fluids. If your urine is dark and your skin or eyes appear yellow, you may have jaundice. Some chemicals found in common medicines can contribute to dark urine. In some cases, excessively dark-coloured urine can signal kidney failure.

- Snoring: Is your partner's snoring giving you sleepless nights but you fear telling him or her to avoid hurting any feelings? Remember that snoring may be an early sign of a sleep disorder called sleep apnea, which can also lead to heart attacks. It is characterised by obstruction in the airways. Sleep apnea can increase risk of pulmonary hypertension and subsequent heart failure.
- Fatigue: While tiredness can be a result of working hard, feeling fatigued constantly can also be an indicator of some serious medical illness. Fatigue can be an indicator of your thyroid not functioning properly. One of the common medical reasons for feeling constantly tired is iron deficiency or anaemia. Chronic fatigue syndrome, also known as myalgic encephalomyelitis (ME), is a severe and disabling tiredness that goes on for at least six months. There are usually other symptoms, such as a sore throat, muscle or joint pain, and headache. Diabetes and prolonged depression might also cause tiredness.
- Stools: It sounds gross that we should be observing the colour, shape or smell of our faeces but the fact is that our stools can clue us into health issues. If your stool is pebbly, you're not getting enough fibre or water in your diet. If it's runny, it could be signs of infection, colitis, food intolerance or allergy. If it's black or red in colour, it could mean that you are overdoing iron supplements or some medications. If it is bloody, that could mean haemorrhoids, rectal bleeding or even cancer. If stools are sticky and gel-like, it could be signs of gastrointestinal

bleeding. If your faeces is light gray or tan in colour, that could mean a minor obstruction in your bile duct or a liver disorder.

An ounce of prevention is worth a pound of cure

So, remember that our body is made in such a remarkable way that it has signalling mechanisms in place to let us know if something is wrong within. However, we have to listen to our body and identify the signals it is sending to warn us about our health condition. Listening to our body is one of the important steps to keep our health at its best. Probably the last time you heard the proverb 'A stitch in time saves nine' was when you were in school. But the wisdom of that proverb is immortal. It is always better to spend your time and energy to deal with a problem right in the beginning than to wait until later, when it worsens and takes longer to deal with.

Consider the case of Shobha. At age sixty-two, she got menstrual bleeding which was way after she had already hit menopause. This was accompanied by frequent urges to use the washroom and there was discharge of an unusual amount with odour. She knew there was something wrong and consulted one of her friends. However, by then her periods had stopped and she was feeling somewhat better. Her friend passed it off as unusual bleeding but Shobha was not convinced. Upon insistence of her daughter-in-law, she went to a gynaecologist for a consultation. The bad news: she was diagnosed with cervical cancer stage 2. The good news: her cancer was diagnosed at an early stage and the chances of recovery were good. She underwent a six-month treatment and today, she is completely out of danger. There are no traces of malignant cells in her body. She gives all credit for her recovery to her daughter-in-law who compelled her to take a medical opinion and treatment in time before it became too late.

Even something as sinister as malignancy can be treated if diagnosed at an early enough time. This is why regular medical check-ups are important. Health tests and screenings can help find problems before they start or at an early stage, when your chances for treatment and cure are better. This ensures that you take steps that help your chances for living a long and healthy life. Now, you can even do a genetic (DNA) test which can tell you about a medical problem you are suffering from even before the symptoms appear or the blood tests reveal an underlying illness. A genetic test can also assess the hidden risk of a medical problem that you might suffer even ten to fifteen years down the line, based on your genetic make-up.

Unfortunately, most of us take our health for granted. We often ignore it while keeping up with the fast pace of life. Most people avoid taking regular health check-ups either due to lack of time or because they feel it is just a waste of money. Some women do not feel guilty spending money on a luxury handbag or vacation but when it comes to spending on their health, they are reluctant to shell out half the amount of money. Let's look at another example:

For eight years, Joana suffered from visual problems, weird sensations in her feet and blisters that would not heal.

However, she ignored these symptoms and would go for only local applications from a nearby pharmacy to fix a problem as and when it occurred. Also, she avoided medical check-ups, as she felt they were unnecessary and a waste of money. She never realised she was in danger until one day she contracted gangrene—a condition that develops when blood cannot travel freely throughout the body, resulting in an infection and death of tissues—in her right foot. She was diagnosed with type 2 diabetes. However, her health had worsened by that time and her leg had to finally be amputated.

Why is it that materialistic things matter to us more than our health? Why do we wait until our body gives up and collapses? Isn't it wise to spend time and money on our health, which is the defining factor of how long and how well we are going to live? At least check for signs that your body sends out as warning signals of something not right within. When you see such symptoms, please do not ignore them. Visit the doctor immediately so that you can correct the problem at an early stage before it worsens beyond repair.

In 2005, Rufina had a heart attack that was partly caused by hypertension. Prior to it, she didn't even know she had the disease, despite having symptoms that indicated there was something wrong within. Nearly 70 per cent of people who have a heart attack have a history of hypertension. For Rufina, it was a scary experience. Just few days before the attack, she had been under a lot of stress due to working continuously for few months in night shifts. She was suffering from headaches for few days that she thought was migraine and attributed to stress. She even took migraine medication but didn't seek medical help. Looking back, she realises that her body was trying to tell her something that she ignored. A few days later, while she was mopping the floor, she felt a sharp pain in her chest. She ignored it, but it woke her up around 3:30 a.m. and she was rushed to the emergency room. She'd had a heart attack. A surgeon performed an angioplasty. When Rufina was discharged from the hospital, part of the diagnosis was hypertension. The stress in her life was a big contributor as well. She also had a family history of hypertension. She realised that if she had paid attention to the signals her body was sending in the form of headaches, and had sought immediate medical help, she may have possibly avoided the heart attack.

How often should you get a medical check-up?

Sometimes your greatest enemy can be inadequate hospital visits for regular medical check-ups. Actually, there is no one size fits all in case of health check-ups. However, if you are under the age of thirty, ordinarily healthy, non-smoker, not overweight and don't take any prescription medicines, you can get a check-up every two to three years. If you are a woman and sexually active, you can get a pap smear to screen for cervical cancer starting at age twenty-one and discuss with your doctor how often you should do it thereafter.

A Chinese proverb says, 'Before thirty, men seek disease; after thirty, disease seeks men.' So, between age thirty and forty, healthy individuals should get a physical check-up every other year and annually after forty. Baseline mammograms are now recommended for women once they turn forty, and should be repeated every one to two years.

It is often joked that life is like a roll of toilet paper—the closer you get to the end, the faster it goes. So unfortunately, annual physical check-ups must become more comprehensive by age fifty. That's also when you should undergo colonoscopies to screen for colon cancer. Repeat every ten years unless there is a family history of colon cancer, colon polyps, or the test results are abnormal.

Some of the main screenings and tests to be included essentially in a regular medical check-up are:

- Cholesterol
- Diabetes
- Blood pressure
- Body mass index (BMI)
- Breast and cervical cancer early detection
- Colorectal cancer screening
- Oral health for adults
- Immunisation schedules
- Prostate cancer screening
- Viral hepatitis
- HIV/AIDS
- Blood tests to evaluate body organs like liver, kidneys, heart and thyroid

The English historian Thomas Fuller rightly remarked, 'He who cures a disease may be the skillfullest, but he that prevents it is the safest physician.' But *you* need to make that happen by taking control. It is not unusual for people only to go to the doctor when they are feeling unwell. However, a regular check-up with your doctor will help him to assess your overall health and to identify your risk factors for disease. By knowing what's normal for you early on, you'll be able to detect any serious risk factors later.

Let me end this chapter on a more positive note. Yes, it is important not to ignore the warning signs. Yes, it is important to seek professional advice in good time. But it is also not a good idea to become a hypochondriac. The English bookseller, William Londen, correctly observed: 'To ensure good health: eat lightly, breathe deeply, live moderately, cultivate cheerfulness, and maintain an interest in life.'

Key Takeaways

- Pay attention to your body. It sends signals if something needs to be fixed within. Remember, a stitch in time saves nine.

- In particular, your hair, skin, oral health, weight, urine colour, snoring, fatigue and stools: they all have hidden indicators of potential illnesses.

- Get medical check-ups at regular frequency according to your age and gender.

- Some of the key markers to consider in these checkups are cholesterol, diabetes, blood pressure, body mass index (BMI), breast and cervical health, colorectal cancer screening, oral health, immunisation schedules, prostate health, viral hepatitis, HIV/AIDS screening and blood tests to evaluate body organs like liver, kidneys, heart and thyroid.

STEP ELEVEN: MODERATE

The British broadcaster Clement Freud once jokingly said, 'If you resolve to give up smoking, drinking and loving, you don't actually live longer; it just seems longer.' In similar vein, Henny Youngman said, 'When I read about the evils of drinking, I gave up reading.' But the truth is far from these witticisms.

Addiction or excess of anything is bad for your health. It could be too much of anything—too much food, too much alcohol, too much exercise… When anything becomes a compulsion, it becomes an addiction that takes over your life.

Why does addiction happen? It is usually due to something that has happened in your life. The triggers can usually be explained by the acronym, HALT. This acronym stands for the four words Hungry, Angry, Lonely and Tired. Look closely and you will find that one of these elements is involved in your behaviour.

How does one recover from an addiction? Most people think that it is by simply stopping doing whatever it is that they are addicted to. They do not realise that actual recovery requires creating a new lifestyle where indulging in the addiction finds no place. The sad truth is that if you do not do this, then all the elements that made you addicted will once again catch up with you.

Let's take a brief look at each type of addiction and see what the health implications are.

Caffeine and drug addiction

Drug addiction leads to terrible consequences in almost every aspect of life—social, financial, emotional, physical. Recognising the signs and symptoms of addiction can prompt earlier intervention and, ultimately, better outcomes.

Drugs can be classified according to the effect that they produce on users. Broadly speaking, there are seven different drug types. Each type has a specific set of characteristics and effects. These are:

- Stimulants: Stimulants influence the body's central nervous system, thus making the user get the feeling of 'speeding up' by pumping up heart rate, blood pressure, breathing and blood glucose. Stimulants may be in pill form but are also consumed by snorting or even mixed into food or drink. For example, caffeine is routinely a stimulant in many beverages and cocaine is usually a fine powder that is snorted. Examples of stimulants include adderall, ritalin, synthetic marijuana, cocaine, methamphetamine, ecstasy and caffeine. Stimulant abuse can create dangerous consequences. These

include anxiety, paranoia, psychosis, very high body temperature, depression, heart failure, stroke and even seizures.
- Depressants: Depressants also effect the body's central nervous system but in a manner opposite to stimulants. These drugs make users feel as though their world is 'slowing down' and thus are also called 'downers'. Doctors often prescribe drugs in this category to help with anxiety, insomnia and OCD. These drugs often offer a sedative experience to users, making them a tempting choice for teens who wish to escape everyday stresses. Examples of depressants are rohypnol, barbiturates, xanax, valium and benziodiazepines. Alcohol also works as a depressant. Depressant abuse can lead to high blood sugar, diabetes and weight gain, increased body temperature, delirium, sluggish thinking, low blood pressure, memory impairment and even hallucinations.
- Hallucinogens: Hallucinogens interfere with communication inside the brain. They cause briskly shifting emotions and perceptions that are unreal. For example, a hallucinogen user may believe that he is being punched by a person who does not even exist. Hallucinogens come in several forms that can be smoked, drunk, eaten or swallowed as pills. Examples are LSD, psilocybin and peyote. Hallucinogen abuse can last a lifetime. Users often deal with unexplainable bouts of fear, paranoia, distorted cognition, anxiety, psychosis, elevated blood pressure and nausea.
- Dissociatives: Dissociatives warp the user's perception

of reality by causing users to 'dissociate' or imagine that they are observing themselves from outside their bodies. Often, dissociatives give users a false sense of invincibility that leads them to undertake risky behaviour such as rash driving, walking on a high ledge or playing with fire. Dissociatives disrupt the brain's glutamate receptors that play an important role in cognition, emotions and pain perception. Common dissociatives are ketamine, dextromethorphan or DXM, phencyclidine or PCP. The immediate effects of disocciatives include depression, anxiety, suicidal thoughts, speech impairment, social withdrawal, hallucinations, numbness, memory loss and detachment from reality.

- Opioids: Opioids are potent painkillers that tend to create a sense of euphoria in users. Mostly drawn from the poppy plant, opioids are sometimes prescribed by doctors for patients in intense pain. The problem is that opioids are habit-forming, often causing addiction within seventy-two hours. DXM is a common opioid ingredient in cough and cold medicines. Often, teenagers take huge doses of cough medicine to get high. Opioids can be smoked, eaten, drunk, injected or swallowed as pills. Examples include heroin, morphine, hydrocodone, opium, vicodin, oxycontin, percocet and codeine. The terrible effects of opioid withdrawal include flu-like symptoms, constipation, liver damage, brain impairment, euphoria, drowsiness, pupil dilation and cardiac arrest.
- Inhalants: These are fumes of everyday household items

that can be inhaled to generate brief feelings of euphoria. Examples of inhalants include marker fumes, paint and paint thinner fumes, gasoline and glue, nitrous oxide, aerosol sprays, and room deodorisers. Inhalant abuse can have serious consequences both short-term and long-term. These include loss of smell, brain damage, nosebleeds, weakness, euphoria, accelerated heart rate, loss of consciousness, hallucinations and impaired speech.

- Cannabis: Cannabis acts like a hallucinogen but also creates effects of a depressant. While it has high potential for addiction, it is also being increasingly used as a medicinal drug in the United States. Unfortunately, marijuana is usually abused by those who do not need it for medical reasons. Cannabis can be smoked, vapourised, drunk or eaten. Examples are marijuana leaves, hashish and hash oil, charas, ganja, bhang and cannabis-derived medicines like sativex. Cannabis abuse has severe implications. These include lowered immunity, depression, anxiety, reduced sperm count, impaired reaction time and sense of time.

Please understand that there is nothing like 'moderation' when it comes to drugs. Any drug user will eventually become addicted, hence the safest bet is to stay away. A witty view is that 'Man does not live by coffee alone. Have a muffin.' The rejoinder to that is: do not get addicted to either.

Digital addiction

Gone are the days when we worried only about addiction to alcohol, cigarettes or drugs. Today, parents are also worrying about addiction to technology, fast food, binge television-watching, compulsive dieting and much more. A host of modern addictions are emerging that reflect the changing ways we live in and the increasing importance we put on certain modern activities.

Digital addiction has bitten not only children but adults as well. India has the world's second highest number of mobile phone users, above one billion at last count. Around 79 per cent of the population between the age groups of eighteen and forty-four have their cell phones with them almost all the time, with only two hours of their waking day spent without their cell phones in hand. Would it surprise you to know that our brains actually get a hit of dopamine and serotonin—the chemicals linked to happiness—when our phones beep or ring? These are the same chemicals that give drug users their 'high'! Let's consider an example:

A couple of years ago, Shefali, a mother of six-year-old Aarav would proudly tell her friends about her son using cell phones so efficiently that the parents would not have to even tell him how to open and close a particular app, a game or even a YouTube video. He would do it himself. Today, she is making her son take treatment to get rid of his addiction to cell phones! It came as a shock to her when a few days ago little Aarav refused to eat food and do homework without his cell phone. He insisted on playing games and watching YouTube videos even before going to bed or before going for a bath. He didn't like playing with his friends and would always be busy with his mobile phone even at birthday parties. Something that started as a distraction strategy to make him eat his food as an infant had become his obsession. Parents, who were proud about their child being so tech-savvy, suddenly found themselves concerned about his health and his studies, which were being affected by his cell phone addiction.

Undoubtedly, technology has enabled us to do things that were previously beyond imagination. However, overuse as well as misuse of technology has also led to the show of unimaginable feats of stupidity. For example, did you know that in India, 41 per cent people use phones for work-related purposes while driving; 60 per cent people do not stop at a safe location before answering calls and 20 per cent people have had a near-miss or a crash due to use of mobile phones while driving?

Overuse of technology has given rise to a sedentary lifestyle and concentration problems in children and adults. Games such as Blue Whale, Pokemon and Fortnight are the latest examples of technology addiction. According to a study done by a Mumbai-based hospital, about 50 per cent of Indian children and teenagers are prone to spinal problems due to the high usage of mobile phones. The problem may lead to permanent damage to their cervical spines that could lead to lifelong pain.

A report published by the Royal Society for Public Health in the UK examined the effects of social media on young people's mental health. According to the report, the popular social media sites Facebook and Instagram negatively impact body image and sleep, increase bullying and 'FOMO' (Fear Of Missing Out), and lead to greater feelings of anxiety, depression and loneliness. The other health hazards of digital addiction are:

- Text neck: The term is used to describe the neck pain and physical damage sustained from the overuse of one's mobile phone, tablet or other wireless devices.
- Backward curve: Due to the overuse of our phones, instead of a normal forward curve, patients are seen to have a backward curve, which can be degenerative, often causing head, neck, shoulder and back pain.
- Behavioural changes: Overuse of technology can also result in emotional and behavioural changes as the stress can affect the release of happy hormones.

So, how much is too much? While adults should be mature enough to know their limits to use technology, the latest guidelines from the American Academy of Paediatrics (AAP) for technology use in children suggest that:

- Children under eighteen months should avoid screen time, other than video-chatting.
- Children aged eighteen months to two years can watch or use high-quality programmes or apps if adults watch or play with them to help them understand what they're seeing.
- Children aged two to five years should have no more than one hour a day of screen time with adults watching or playing with them.

- Children aged six years and older should have consistent limits on the time they spend on electronic media and the types of media they use.

Taiwanese parents are now legally obligated to monitor their children's screen time. The government there can levy £1,000 fine on parents of children under the age of eighteen who are using electronic devices for extended periods of times. Similar measures have been adopted in China and South Korea that aim to limit screen time to a healthy level.

Work addiction

One of the Hollywood divas rightly observed, 'The ideal man doesn't smoke, doesn't drink, doesn't take drugs, doesn't swear, doesn't cheat, doesn't get angry, doesn't exist.' She would never have imagined including work in that particular list. Consider this example:

Mihir, one of my patients, worked as a marketing manager at one of the top telecom companies in India. When he came to me for treatment, he complained about being depressed. He said he didn't even know what was causing so much of stress in him. However, it was affecting his physical health and led to a disturbance in his personal life. His girlfriend broke up with him and his mother complained of being unable to cope with his angry outbursts. He started smoking and suffered from sudden chest pains and became anxious before making presentations at office.

After talking to him more about his personal and professional life, I realised that Mihir was an extremely ambitious young man and wanted to achieve great heights professionally—nothing wrong with that. However, I noticed the fact that his ambitions were far from being realistic. Mihir was trying to achieve success by putting in too much of time and investing more than the required amount of energy in his work. Because of this, he was losing sleep, was increasingly getting obsessed with work-related success, had an intense fear of failure and was paranoid about work-related performances. Through all this, he ignored his personal life and health.

Yes, addiction to work is a mental condition. Much like someone with a drug addiction, a person who has work addiction achieves a 'high' from working more than normal. This leads him to keep repeating this behaviour. Such people are unable to change despite realising the negative ways it affects their personal life and their physical and mental health.

How do you know if you are a work addict?

- You are always on the lookout on how you can engage yourself more in work.
- You work in order to reduce guilt, feelings of helplessness or depression and anxiety.
- Despite requests from friends and family to reduce your work time, you invest more than the required time at office.
- You spend your time at home, too, working.
- You spend much more time working than you intended to do at the start of the day.
- You become stressed when you are not able to work.

- You do not give time to your hobbies, fun activities and fitness, and instead put all that time in work.
- You work so much that it has negatively impacted your health and your relationships.

If you have any of the above symptoms, you need to take medical treatment, as work addiction, too, needs to be treated like any other form of addiction. Treat it before it takes a toll on your health and personal life.

Nicotine addiction

The novelist and playwright Somerset Maugham joked, 'It's very easy to leave smoking. I've left it ten times.' He was driving home the point that this is one of the most addictive substances known to man.

Nicotine is an addictive substance which is primarily ingested through the lungs. The compulsive need to continue smoking is the result of nicotine dependence. Many countries have now substantially increased taxes on tobacco-related items and also spent money on anti-smoking campaigns. Some nations have laws banning smoking in public places.

The dangers of smoking are well-documented. Smoking makes it twenty-five times more likely that an individual will eventually develop lung cancer. In fact, smoking can cause cancer in almost every part of the body, not just the lungs. It also increases the odds of death if cancer does occur. Those with asthma find that smoking aggravates it or triggers attacks. Smokers also have a much higher risk of angina, peripheral vascular disease, stroke or heart attack.

Just five cigarettes a day can elevate the risk of cardiovascular diseases, including Buerger's disease, a condition that causes dangerous clotting. Women who smoke have a higher probability of infertility and male smokers have a higher risk of erectile dysfunction. Smoking during a pregnancy can seriously harm mothers and the developing foetus. Smoking increases insulin resistance and enhances the odds of developing type-2 diabetes. Also, diabetics who smoke are more likely to experience complications than diabetics who do not. On average, smokers live ten years less than non-smokers. Smoking substantially increases the risk of sudden death.

The root cause of nicotine addiction is the addictive nature of nicotine. It elevates the supply of neurotransmitters—the ones that regulate behaviour and mood. These are dopamine and noradrenaline. Smokers crave the neurotransmitter rush that enhances mood and concentration. When a person does not smoke for a few hours, these hormone levels drop. This, in turn, triggers anxiety and irritability prompting the smoker to light up yet another cigarette. This urge can be more pronounced at certain times of the day—after morning coffee or with a drink at the pub.

Quitting smoking can improve your life by giving you a slower heart rate, lower blood carbon monoxide levels, improved lung function within ninety days, improved blood circulation and lowered risk of heart attack, and reduced risk of stroke within five to fifteen years. Thus the benefits of quitting are immense. Some tips that can enable you to stop:

- Determine the triggers that cause you to smoke. This will help you understand why you are reaching for that cigarette.
- Family, friends, colleagues can help you stop. It is necessary to be honest and explain the importance of their assistance.
- Pay attention to the positive rather than negative. Look at quitting as liberation rather than sacrifice.
- If there are people around you who smoke, arrive at an amicable arrangement so that your ability to quit long-term is not diminished.
- Read and re-read the list of reasons why you are giving up smoking to perpetually remember the need to do it.
- Treat yourself as you reach milestones.
- Find other ways to relieve stress—exercise is a good option.
- When you experience craving, take a deep breath and visualise your lungs drawing in fresh air. Remind yourself of the benefits.
- Remember that cravings are temporary. Take a ten-minute break from whatever you are doing to allow yourself to move beyond the immediate craving.

Some smokers switch to vapes and e-cigarettes in their quest to quit. These nicotine delivery approaches have less harmful effects than traditional smoking but they cannot help a person fight nicotine addiction unless such switching is a temporary part of a larger cessation plan. Treating nicotine dependence is aimed at reducing withdrawal symptoms and finding ways to deal with the psychological urges. There are several medications and therapies available today to assist in quitting. For example, nicotine replacement therapy (NRT) is a way of ingesting nicotine without smoking. NRT releases nicotine into your bloodstream at reduced doses vis-à-vis tobacco smoke. The reduced but steady supply can possibly negate the cravings associated with quitting. Examples of NRT include nicotine patches, nicotine gum, nicotine lozenges, nicotine inhalers and nicotine nasal sprays. There are also medications such as varenicline, clonidine and bupropion to treat nicotine dependence. While medicines may alleviate the immediate physical problems associated with quitting, it is behavioural therapy that usually helps people remain smoke-free on a long-term basis.

Relationship, sexual and porn addictions

People are today also seeking treatment for their out of control romantic and/or sexual behaviours, which is either love addiction, relationship addiction or sex addiction. These individuals are most often not sure about how to label their problem. The confusion stems from the fact that all these addictions manifest in similar and sometimes interrelated ways, making it difficult to distinguish one from another.

How do you know if your partner is a love addict? Addicts love their partners with extreme intensity that is neither in their interest nor in the best interest of their partner. Typically, they are so obsessed with their partners that they push aside their own needs and focus on fulfilling the needs and wants of the other person to the exclusion of everything else. Love addicts measure their self-worth based on how much someone else seems to want or need them. By ignoring their own needs, they choose to compulsively focus on the other person, using that person's opinion about them as their primary, and sometimes *only*, source of validation.

Relationship addicts, on the other hand, are preoccupied to the point of obsession not with a single partner, as love addicts are, but with the idea of falling in love, with different partners. While love addicts focus on a single long-term relationship, relationship addicts keep on bouncing from one relationship to another. They put in a tremendous amount of time and energy on romance—hooking partners, looking for a new partner, escaping one relationship to pursue another, and juggling multiple relationships simultaneously, to an extent that they cause damage to most of their relationships and to themselves.

Sex addicts are so obsessed with sex that they tend to focus only on their sexual experience rather than a person or their relationship. Highly objectified sexual fantasies as well as the pursuit of sexual activity control their thinking so much that they easily cheat on their partners to have sexual pleasures elsewhere. Most of their time is consumed by either watching pornography videos or fantasising about sexual activity even when they are in the middle of work or conversation. Their behaviour eventually leads to damaged relationships, trouble at work, depression, social and emotional isolation, loss of self-esteem, financial loss and physical ailments.

How to spot sexual addiction? It could manifest as one or more of these signs:

- Sex dominates a person's life to the exclusion of other activities.
- A sex addict often engages in various acts like phone sex, computer sex, visiting prostitutes, pornography or exhibitionism.
- A person habitually masturbates, at times at places which are not appropriate.
- An individual has multiple sexual partners or cheats on partners.
- In extreme cases, the person engages in criminal activities, including stalking, rape, incest or child molestation.

Alcohol addiction

Rodney Dangerfield, the irrepressible American comic, once joked, 'I drink too much. The last time I gave a urine sample it had an olive in it.' Do you have a similar problem?

Alcohol addiction—often referred to as alcoholism—is a disease. While researchers are trying to identify the factors that may increase the odds of alcoholism—genetics, race and socio-economic position—the truth is that we still do not know what causes it. Alcoholism is a real disease. It eventually brings about significant modifications to the brain and neurochemistry. Thus, an alcoholic may eventually become incapable of controlling his actions.

Alcohol addiction manifests in different ways. The seriousness of the condition, the frequency of drinking, and the nature of alcohol that is consumed differs from one person to the next. For example, some people drink through the day, while other alcoholics may binge drink and then sober up for an interval of time. Irrespective of the nature of the alcohol addiction, it may be safely said that you have an alcohol addiction if you rely on drinking and cannot stay sober for an extended period of time.

There are several health complications associated with alcoholism. These include ulcers, diabetes, sexual dysfunction, birth defects, bone loss, liver damage, vision problems, elevated risk of cancer and lower immune function.

What are the symptoms of alcoholism? Alcohol addiction is often extremely tricky and difficult to recognise. Unlike cocaine or heroin, alcohol is part of social celebrations and is linked intimately to celebration. When something is common in society, it can often be difficult to spot the difference between a casual drinker and an alcoholic. Some symptoms of alcohol addiction are higher quantity of alcohol or greater frequency in use, changes in social circle and opting for friends who are drinkers, greater dependence on alcohol to get through regular life, absence of hangover symptoms, consumption at inappropriate times or places, avoiding contact with friends or family, increased depression, lethargy, emotional outbursts and avoiding events where alcohol is absent.

Treating alcohol addiction is often challenging. The first step must necessarily involve the alcoholic wanting to get sober. The success of any programme depends on the individual's desire to get better. Also, the recovery process implies a lifetime commitment. There isn't any quick fix because the probability of a relapse is always high. An initial treatment option for alcohol addiction is an outpatient or inpatient rehab programme that can last from thirty days to a year. Such a programme helps alcoholics handle withdrawal symptoms. Another option is twelve-step programmes like Alcoholics Anonymous (AA).

Paan and gutka addiction

Gutka is a combination of areca nut, slaked lime, paraffin and katechu along with tobacco. Gutka is said to have stimulant and relaxation effects but many oncologists say that it is highly carcinogenic. Gutka usually contains compounds of nitorsamines, arsenic and benzopyrenes apart from chemicals closely associated with chlorine and ammonium compounds. It also contains carbon monoxide, sulphur dioxide and hydrocarbons.

Gutka use has been linked to cancers of mouth, throat, lung and oesophagus. Besides cancer, users can develop non-cancerous conditions like bronchial asthma, hypertension, heart disease and stroke. Narrowing of the blood vessels can cause gangrene, stoppage of blood supply and low birth weight babies. Less sinister effects are loss of appetite, unusual sleep patterns and loss of concentration.

Moderation is key

There are several other addictions including food and sugar addiction, exercise addiction and even shopping addiction. Nowadays, the standard advice is 'everything in moderation' and this principle is apparently applicable to everything—eating, drinking, working, sleeping and even loving. But how much is really too much? And how much is too little? There are some things that you simply need to give up entirely. You can't 'moderate' drugs or nicotine. But there are other things that you can.

Most doctors have held that drinking a little bit is good for your health. So for every study that correlates alcohol to liver disease, there is another suggesting that moderate use results in lowered stress levels and reduced risk of heart disease. What should you do? Probably the best path is to stick to consuming no more than one drink a day. This would enable you to lower your risk and take advantage of some stress reduction. Henny Youngman famously joked, 'My grandmother is over eighty and still doesn't need glasses. Drinks right out of the bottle.' There is no reason why moderate drinking should come in the way of a long life. Personally, I believe that the social impact of drinking is worse than the medical impact of it. Stealing money to drink, abuse and violence at homes are some examples of adverse social impact of drinking.

The same principle applies to exercise. Aggressively increasing cardio may help some people but way too much of any one sort of exercise can lead to health problems and overuse injuries. Examples are pain or inflammation in joints and connective tissues. So, how much should you exercise? If your cardio is a brisk walk or a bike ride, it would be a good idea to get thirty minutes five days per week. But if exercise means a spinning class or hiking, then twenty minutes three days per week might do the trick. The moderation trick is to mix in weight training, stretching or yoga on non-cardio days to enhance the payoff.

What about caffeine? Again, there's no simple answer. On average, most Americans consume 165 milligrams of 'liquid caffeine' per day. That's actually half of the 400 milligrams that the US Food & Drug Administration terms as 'reasonable'. In fact, there are several studies that link moderate caffeine usage with reduced risk of cancer, stroke risk, Parkinson's disease, fatty liver, heart disease and chronic inflammation. We mostly think of caffeine as the morning cup of coffee but it is in many other sources including sodas, chocolate, medications, dietary supplements, energy drinks and tea. Overdone, caffeine can alter behaviour processes such as mood and activity level and excessive use of caffeine can lead to severe withdrawal symptoms when it is stopped. Limiting one's daily intake to one to two cups or consuming decaf is the wise move.

How much sleep should you get? Seven to eight hours per day is usually adequate for most adults. But you know what, losing sleep one night to binge-watch your favourite Netflix show isn't going to kill you. You will be less attentive the next day but your body will compensate over the next couple of nights. The problem is if you repeat this behaviour several times each week. According to a study in *Occupational & Environmental Medicine*, a nineteen-hour waking stint can leave you as cognitively impaired as a drunk person. Shortage of sleep can eventually result in obesity and cardiovascular risk. What's funny is that oversleeping can have the same effects.

Let's then consider digital moderation. We check our phones for texts, emails, replies and likes around sixty times a day (that's about once every fifteen minutes while we're awake) according to a study at California State University. That's about four hours of screen time each day which is double the amount that's acceptable. To unplug, you can try setting no-phone zones at the dinner table, at the gym and in bed. Eventually you will be able to cut your usage time to half.

What about food? A broad thumb rule is that less than 10 per cent of your daily calorie intake should come from added sugar. You'll be surprised that it's there in virtually everything—yoghurt, juice, soda, even ketchup. Eat too much sugar and the risk of obesity, type-2 diabetes and cardiovascular disease shoots up. Fad diets change from time to time, but limit saturated fats to 10 per cent of your diet and all fats to less than a third. Try to get at least fifty grams of protein in the day. And look out for that other killer, sodium. Most of us consume around 3,400 milligrams per day vis-à-vis the ideal 1,500.

The cross-country skier, Herman Smith-Johannsen, once offered his mantra to a good life: 'Stay busy, get plenty of exercise, and don't drink too much. Then again, don't drink too little.' And that pretty much sums up moderation. Take everything in moderation—including moderation.

> ### KEY TAKEAWAYS
>
> - Addiction is usually triggered by you being hungry, angry, lonely or tired.
>
> - Drug addiction can include stimulants, depressants, hallucinogens, dissociatives, opioids, inhalants and cannabis. There is nothing like moderation when it comes to drugs. Every user will eventually get addicted and so it's best to stay away.
>
> - Digital addiction is affecting children and adults. Create no-technology hours and zones to avoid addiction.
>
> - Work addiction is real. It is the 'high' achieved from extra work. It eventually can take a toll on your health and family life.
>
> - Nicotine is one of the most addictive substances known to man. There are many possibilities these days to quit the habit with the support of nicotine patches, gum, inhalers and sprays.

- Relationship, sexual and porn addiction also call for counselling or lifestyle changes.
- Rehabilitation from alcohol addiction requires a lifetime commitment and involves lifestyle changes along with group support such as AA.
- The key lies in moderation—be it food, alcohol, exercise, caffeine, sleep or digital.

STEP TWELVE: RELAX

Stress is part of life—be it minor hassles such as the morning traffic rush or the irritable boss or more serious issues such as the health of a loved one or a messy divorce. Irrespective of the reasons, stress results in a rush of hormones such as cortisol into your bloodstream. This leads to increased heart rate, tensed muscles and quicker and shallower breathing. This inevitable 'stress response' is the result of genetic programming hardwired into us from prehistory—ostensibly to help us react intelligently to natural disasters and predators.

While we can't avoid the triggers that cause stress in our lives, we can determine far better ways of reacting to them. As basketball coach Dean Smith said, 'If you treat every situation as a life and death matter, you'll die a lot of times.' One possible method to avoid dying often is to set off what is known as the 'relaxation response'. It is the reverse of the stress response. It is a condition of intense rest that can be stimulated in various ways. With steady training, you can create a reservoir of calm that you can access whenever the need arises. The relaxation response was first outlined by

Dr Herbert Benson in the 1970s, at the Harvard Medical School. Some of his suggested approaches are outlined below.

The relaxation response

According to Dr Benson, broadly, there are six relaxation techniques that can assist in triggering the calmness that you desire and thus lower stress. These are:

- Breath focus: This method is simple yet exceedingly powerful. All you need to do is to take slow, long and deep breaths. This is also sometimes called abdominal breathing. This is accompanied by uncoupling your mind from diverting ideas, thoughts, emotions and sensations. Within this book is a chapter on breathing (See *Step Seven: Breathe*). Please review it to understand some of the deep breathing and meditation techniques outlined.
- Body scan: This method combines breath focus with increasing muscle relaxation. Once you are settled into the rhythm of deep breathing, you focus your attention on one part of the body or one group of muscles. Parallelly, you mentally let go of any physical tension that you may be experiencing there. This is very similar to the Buddhist vipassana technique. A body scan also promotes a deeper and more intimate appreciation of the connection between body and mind.
- Mindfulness meditation: This involves sitting upright in a comfortable position and focusing on your breath. Every breath forces you to bring your attention to the

present moment without wandering into the usual worries about the past or the future. Mindfulness meditation is gaining popularity these days and recent research seems to indicate that it may be useful in dealing with anxiety, depression and pain.
- Guided imagery: In this method you imagine calming scenes, locations or experiences within your mind that can assist you to relax. These days, you can also find apps and videos of calming scenes and sounds. Always ensure that you choose pictures and sounds that you personally find soothing because tastes vary across users.
- Repetitive prayer or chanting: Practitioners of this method silently repeat a short prayer, phrase or mantra while remaining focused on breath. This method has worked for monks and spiritual practitioners down the ages. It may be ideal for you if you are are religiously or spiritually inclined.
- Yoga, tai chi and qigong: These are three ancient techniques that combine rhythmic breath with physical movements. The physical element involved in these methods can sometimes be the perfect distraction from rapid thoughts.

Experts suggest that you should cycle through several methods to determine which one works for you. The overall results of relaxation cannot be adequately stressed. These include:

- Lowered heart rate
- Reduced blood pressure

- Slower and deeper breathing
- Enhanced digestion
- Normalcy in blood sugar levels
- Lowered stress hormones
- Better blood flow to major muscles
- Reduced muscle tension and chronic pain
- Improved concentration and mood
- Reduced insomnia
- Reduced fatigue
- Lesser anger and irritability
- Boosted confidence

There are a few more relaxation techniques that are not mentioned in Dr Benson's study. Those are outlined below.

Massage therapy

Massage therapy is an option that was once viewed as 'alternative' or 'fringe' but that is no longer the case. Massage is a mainstream approach to relaxation. Massage therapy can be of different types—Swedish massage, Thai massage, Shiatsu, hot stone massage, deep tissue massage, reflexology and so on. Each type of massage works differently towards increasing circulation, relieving tension, lowering stress and anxiety, improving sleep or pain relief in muscles, tendons and connective tissue. Let's examine some of the key benefits of massage therapy:

- Reduces cortisol: Higher stress means elevated levels of cortisol. As we know, cortisol is linked to headaches, weight gain, insomnia and digestion problems. Massage

therapy has been shown to lower cortisol levels thus prompting the body to enter a recovery phase and triggering relaxation and elevated mood.
- Stress buster: Not only does massage therapy lower stress but regular massages over extended timeframes are known to boost energy levels and reduce pain.
- Reduced blood pressure: Some long-term studies have found that a regular massage programme can lower both systolic and diastolic blood pressure. In turn, lowered blood pressure reduces the risk of heart attack, stroke or kidney failure.
- Relaxes muscles: The key objective of massage therapy is to target and bring relief to the source of the body's pain. It achieves this by increasing flexibility and reducing muscle tension. It also boosts circulation to the target muscle groups and thus enhances supply of nutrients and oxygen to those areas.
- Releases endorphins: These are pain-killing hormones which also increase the supply of dopamine and serotonin levels in the body. These hormones collectively promote healing, pain management, calmness and better mood.
- Improves circulation: Improved circulation is part of a chain reaction that happens in your body as the outcome of consistent massage therapy. Improved circulation promotes healing of damaged, stiff or tense muscles. Massage also improves supply of blood to damaged and congested areas of the body thus speeding up healing.
- Removes lactic acid: The squeezing, twisting and pulling action of massage removes lactic acid from muscle tissue. This, in turn, leads to improved lymph circulation

responsible for transporting metabolic waste away from internal organs.
- Helps posture and alignment: Chronic back pain which is the leading cause of absenteeism at work can be alleviated through massage. As part of a regular massage therapy programme, the body's muscles are loosened and relaxed. Eventually the joints are provided greater freedom, flexibility and range of motion besides relieving pressure points. The body is thus made more capable of assuming healthier positions.
- Strengthens immune system: Studies have shown that regular massage can increase the immune system's cytotoxic capacity. These are the body's natural killer cells that fight infection.

Laughter is indeed the best medicine

Sunny, a nineteen-year old from Chandigarh, came all the way to Mumbai along with his ailing mother who had been battling depression for a long time to thank the actors of a popular television comedy show for her speedy recovery. Sunny mentioned that for years, after the death of his father, he had not seen his mother smile or laugh. She looked stressed most times and hardly interacted with anyone at home. While the family was watching this show, he saw his mother smile. Sunny then got recordings of the show and played them for her. Every time she saw it she burst into laughter. The feeling of happiness and laughter became a tool to fight her depression. Her doctor actually wrote on her medical papers: 'Laughter is the best medicine.'

We are all aware of the mood-boosting benefits of a good laugh. However, researchers at California's Loma Linda University have found that good humour can deliver more than just comic relief. The study measured stress levels and the short term memory in twenty healthy adults in their sixties and seventies. One group was asked to sit silently. The participants in that group were not allowed to talk, read or use their cell phones, while the other group watched funny videos. After twenty minutes, the participants were asked to give their saliva samples and a short memory test was taken. The results concluded that while both groups performed better after the break than before, the 'humour group' or the group that watched funny videos and laughed performed significantly better when it came to memory recall. The participants in that group had recall abilities of 43.6 per cent, compared to 20.3 per cent in the non-humour group. Also, the humour group showed considerably low levels of cortisol, the stress hormone, whereas the non-humour group's stress levels decreased just slightly.

Laughing can also aid in weight loss. Surprising but true. Consider this example:

Simi weighed eighty-four kilos at nineteen years of age. She felt hungry most of the time and would impulsively reach out for junk food and chocolate to satisfy her hunger pangs. She tried hard to cut out junk food from her diet but was unable to do so. She would often feel guilty after eating. Sarcastic remarks on her weight from friends and family made her feel sad and she would end up eating more to cope with those comments. Nothing really motivated her to exercise or eat healthy. Everything changed one day when she made a new friend, Ashok. He was a classmate who had a wonderful sense of humour and kept her laughing throughout the day with his jokes and witty remarks. They would often spend hours together and Simi found herself laughing through the day. Soon she realised that her impulses to eat junk food and sugar-coated candies had reduced considerably. By the end of one year from the day she met Ashok, Simi had lost twelve kilos. Her doctor told her, 'The reason for your weight loss is laughter and happiness.'

You might ask how laughter and being happy can burn calories. This happens because people are less likely to choose impulsively if they have higher levels of serotonin. Because you have greater control on your impulses, you make wiser food choices. A study by Vanderbilt University has estimated that just ten to fifteen minutes of laughter a day can burn as much as forty calories. Another study by Dr Helen Pilcher found that an hour of strong laughter burns off around hundred calories—same as the calories burnt through half-an-hour of weightlifting. Laughter gives the body a 'mini aerobic workout'. It causes the heart to beat faster and send larger amounts of blood around the body. Also, when you laugh out loud, it makes the chest rise and fall, which means that stomach muscles work harder thus helping tighten them. The act of laughing can even help the skin, by using up to fifteen facial muscles that helps to give the face a workout.

Amazingly, the quickest way to lower your blood pressure is to just watch or read something funny. Laughter and humour can lower systolic blood pressure—the top number—by about ten points in just twenty minutes. A growing number of healthcare organisations across the world are now making humour and laughter a part of their treatment protocol. In my practice, I have seen that patients who had the will to live had a sense of humour and were able to use their humour in fighting their illnesses. A positive attitude, a happy mood and a good sense of humour can add years to your lives. As book publisher Judith Regan says, 'The key to successful aging is to pay as little attention to it as possible.'

Other techniques

There are many other relaxation techniques that are available to us. Without getting into too much detail, I am outlining some of those that are being increasingly used these days.

- Hydrotherapy: This is also called balneotherapy and involves the use of water in any form or at any temperature—steam, liquid or ice—for healing. Water has been part of medicinal treatment for many centuries by several cultures including those of ancient China, Japan, India, Rome, Greece, the Americas and the Middle East. Modern hydrotherapy owes its origins to the creation of 'water cure' spas in nineteenth century Europe. These therapies include immersion, wet towel, douches, hip baths, steam treatments, whirlpools, hot tubs and mineral baths. As poet Sylvia Plath once wittily said, 'There must be quite a few things that a hot bath won't cure, but I don't know many of them.'

- Aromatherapy: Aromatherapy is simply the use of scent derived from essential oils, to enhance your psychological and physical well-being. The use of frankincense, camphor, sandalwood and many other smells in places of worship down the centuries is part of the same theory. Your aromatherapy consultant can figure out the best aroma (or combination of various aromas) for you and then use that to relax you. Some of the most commonly used essential oils are bergamot, chamomile, jasmine, lavender, marjoram, rose, valerian and vetiver.
- Music and art therapy: Art and music have the ability to produce a powerful release of feelings that can be healing to the mind, body and spirit. Art and music therapy is said to promote relaxation and stress relief, allow emotions to the fore, improve memory, lower blood pressure and encourage communication between loved ones. It is also helpful for those who are grieving.
- Biofeedback: Biofeedback therapy is used to help prevent or treat conditions, including migraine headaches, stress, chronic pain, incontinence and high blood pressure. The biofeedback theory is that you can use your mind to become more aware of what's happening inside your body and thus gain control over your health. During a biofeedback session, electrodes are attached to your skin and fingers. These sensors are able to capture data on your heart and breathing rate, blood pressure, skin temperature, sweating or muscle activity. The biofeedback therapist helps you fine-tune

relaxation routines. For example, you might use a relaxation process to mute the brainwaves that activate when you have a headache.

The philosopher Jiddu Krishnamurthy rightly said, 'Most of us are frightened of dying because we don't know what it means to live.' It's time to start living and the first step is learning to relax.

Key Takeaways

- Stress results in a rush of hormones such as cortisol into your bloodstream. This leads to increased heart rate, tensed muscles and quicker and shallower breathing.

- While we can't avoid the triggers that cause stress in our lives, we can determine far better ways of reacting to them.

- One of the ways is the relaxation response—this includes breath focus, body scan, mindfulness meditation, guided imagery, chanting, yoga or tai chi.

- Other methods include massage therapy, laughter therapy, hydrotherapy, aromatherapy, music and art therapy, and biofeedback.

STEP THIRTEEN: REJOICE

'Contentment is the way to happiness.' How many times have we heard this particular statement? There is also the old Irish proverb that says, 'A good laugh and a long sleep are the best cures in the doctor's book.' But how many of us realise that being happy or unhappy has a significant impact on our health? Robert Holden, considered to be the UK's leading expert on happiness, says, 'There is no true health without happiness.' People who are unhappy easily fall victim to negative emotions like stress and anxiety. This affects their health, as many illnesses are an outcome of being stressed or anxious. So if we want to feel better and improve our health, we should start focusing on the things that bring us happiness. But we first need to understand what is meant by happiness before we can strive towards achieving it.

Contentment

When I ask my patients what they want out of life, they say that they want to be happy. But when I ask them what happiness means for them, they have difficulty defining it. They can't remember the last time they were happy in many years. What they lack is actually the ability to understand the difference between contentment and happiness. If happiness is the house you want to build, contentment is the foundation for constructing that house. You simply can't build the house without the foundation.

Unfortunately, happiness and success are measured today in terms of bank balance, houses, cars, business, social connections and lifestyle. It is the reason why we focus on ambition—a larger this, higher that, bigger this, more luxurious that. We put in long and exhausting hours to make more money but often fail, thus becoming unhappy. While there is nothing wrong with having milestones, it is important to understand the importance of contentment while achieving these milestones. Money or possessions do not bring lasting happiness, but contentment does.

According to the *Journal of Happiness Studies*, once our basic needs are met, more money does little to improve our overall happiness or our sense of well-being. Does that mean we can have a lazy outlook towards life and be content with whatever we have without striving for a better life? Certainly not. Being content is not being unambitious. Simply be thankful for the life you have while fighting for the life you want. That sums up contentment. Let's look at a real life example:

Nikhil was going through one of the most difficult phases in his life. He had lost his job. He had a wife, two children and an aging mother to support in addition to paying monthly installments on a home loan. He was desperately searching for a job but none suitable for his qualifications and calibre had appeared. He kept his family in the dark but the pressure forced him into excessive smoking and drinking. He often entertained suicidal thoughts to end his misery. One day while he was on his way back home from a job interview, Nikhil met one of his affluent college buddies, Raj. Raj invited him home for lunch. Nikhil was taken aback by Raj's humble lifestyle. He had lost his father two years ago and also his business in a family dispute. He no longer stayed in his family bungalow but lived in a modest 1BHK apartment with his family. Raj revealed that he had been weeks without income. He had even made his kids drop out from school because he could not make ends meet. Raj told Nikhil that his family had been his biggest support in those testing times. He was now earning enough to provide his family a respectable life and his kids were back in school. He was also fighting a legal battle for his business and property and was on the verge of winning. Everything had been possible due to the love and support of his family. That day Nikhil realised the importance of valuing what he had. He went home, gathered the courage to tell his wife about his situation but also assured her that he would work towards turning the tide with her help. Nikhil's family jumped in to support him. His confidence grew and he doubled his efforts to search for a job, and finally got one. There was no looking back for Nikhil thereafter.

Contentment is not fulfillment of what you want; rather, it is the realisation of what you have. It means learning to make the best of the resources available in life. It should provide you with the positivity and zeal to move ahead. On the other hand, discontentment results in feelings like jealously, comparison, impatience, depression, inadequacy and aggression. These are sure triggers for unhappiness. It damages our lives in ways that are irreparable. We have all heard the story of the man who kept complaining about his lack of shoes until he came across another who had no feet.

Emotional health is often ignored to great peril

When we suffer from backache, toothache, chest pain, cold, fever or any other physical health problem, we immediately seek medical help. But how many of us visit a doctor when we feel depressed, stressed, anxious or emotionally drained? Not many, because we feel embarrassed to seek help for these issues. We view these conditions as 'weaknesses' which we should handle ourselves and not let others know about.

It should come as no surprise that India is the most depressed country in the world according to the World Health Organisation (WHO). At 36 per cent, we have the highest rate of depression as also the highest suicide rate in the world. Over one lakh people on an average kill themselves in India every year and these are only the reported figures of suicide due to depression. The harsh truth is we often fail to understand that our physical and emotional health is interrelated. It's time we realise that seeking medical help for emotional problems is not a sign of weakness but as important as seeking help for any other health problem.

Actress Deepika Padukone was amongst few celebrities who dared to go public about her struggles with depression. In one of her interviews, she emphasised the fact that most people with emotional health problems including depression do not show any symptoms. It is therefore difficult to know that they are fighting a difficult battle. She mentioned, 'Back in 2014, when I was in pain, I suffered alone, and used to break down repeatedly. I didn't even know I was depressed. I was going about my day, posing for cameras, getting interviewed and signing autographs. But what nobody saw was that I didn't feel like myself, I felt 'different' somehow. My breathing was irregular and shallow, my stomach was in knots, getting out of bed was a struggle and I would break down for no reason. All I wanted to do was to curl up and stay in bed.' Luckily for Deepika, her mother understood that Deepika's behaviour was more than just passing sadness and got her the help she required. Thanks to timely expert intervention, love and support of her family and friends that Deepika was able to treat her depression with medication, therapy and lifestyle changes.

Emotional illnesses *can* be treated effectively with proper and timely medical intervention. What is the need of the hour is to de-stigmatise and create awareness about such emotional illnesses while encouraging people to seek help for it. Let's take another example, a more ordinary one:

Ishita, a fourteen-year-old teenager visited me seeking treatment for a rash on her cheek which she had first noticed a month ago. It grew worse by the day and soon she saw a few rashes appearing on other parts of her body as well. That is when she decided to consult me. I diagnosed her condition as neurodermatitis. Having been brought up in a conservative family, Ishita had had a strict upbringing. Her father as the traditional head of the family decided everything at home. That included what clothes Ishita could wear, which friends were appropriate and even the activities that she could participate in. Ishita loved playing badminton but couldn't follow her dream because of the compulsory dress code in the badminton courts of her college. Also, the practice sessions happened in the evenings and she couldn't attend them due to the deadline by which she was required to return home. I found that the cause of her skin irritation was stress. Counselling sessions and medications followed. These were targeted to better mind-body balance. Her father, too, was counselled and he eventually agreed to permit her to pursue badminton after some persuasion. Ishita eventually made a full recovery from her skin condition.

Like poor physical health can put us at risk of developing mental or emotional health problems, poor emotional health can negatively impact our physical health, making us prone to medical disorders. Anger or fear, for example, sets our heart racing and the feeling of happiness makes us smile. Positive emotions have been linked to better health, longer life and greater well-being, whereas negative emotions like anger, worry and hostility increase the risk of developing heart disease, as people react to these feelings with raised blood pressure and stiffening of blood vessels.

Poor emotional health can also weaken your body's immune system. This makes you more likely to get infections like cold and flu during emotionally difficult times. Also, when you feel stressed, anxious or depressed, you end up not taking care of your health as well as you should. In emotionally challenging times, you don't even feel like exercising, eating healthy food or taking timely medication. Often, poor emotional health may prompt you to succumb to alcohol, tobacco or other drugs. In addition it can lead to back pain, change in appetite, chest pain, constipation, diarrhoea, extreme tiredness, body aches and pains, headaches, high blood pressure, insomnia, palpitations, sexual problems, shortness of breath, stiff neck and weight gain or loss.

Sometimes, emotional health is triggered by certain unpleasant events that take place in our life like a break-up, death of a beloved, divorce or a serious illness.

When actor Aamir Khan went through his separation and divorce with his ex-wife Reena, mother of his two kids, Aamir went through a period of extreme emotional upheaval. He took four years off from work during which he dealt with regaining his emotional health by being with himself, his children, and even seeking professional help. In one of his interviews during that time, he said, 'I gave a lot of value to my marriage and felt very emotionally damaged when it broke. I was in no state to work in those years. This was also the time I realised however dedicated I may be to work, at the core I need emotional anchoring; being rooted in family is very important to me.' Only after he regained his emotional health could he focus on his work and happiness on the personal front as well.

The American journalist and author, Norman Cousins, rightly observed, 'Death is not the greatest loss in life. The greatest loss is what dies inside us while we live.' We must do everything in our power to live life to the fullest.

What is meant by being emotionally healthy?

Emotionally healthy people are those who can control their emotions and do not allow those emotions to play on their minds and bodies. If you are emotionally healthy:

- You feel good about yourself.
- You do not become overwhelmed by emotions such as fear, anger, love, jealousy, guilt or anxiety.
- You have lasting and satisfying personal relationships.
- You feel comfortable with other people.
- You can laugh at yourself and with others.
- You have respect for yourself and for others even if there are differences.
- You are able to accept life's disappointments.
- You can meet life's demands and handle problems with resilience.
- You make your own decisions and take responsibility of consequences.
- You shape your environment whenever possible and adjust to it when necessary.

The four ingredients of happiness

One of my friends once said to me, 'I am rich, fit, and I have mastered almost everything I wanted to master. Why am I still not happy?' Are you, too, looking for an answer to this question? The answer lies in the mechanism that causes happiness. Happiness is caused by four chemicals in our bodies. These are endorphins, dopamine, oxytocin and serotonin.

- When we want to become fit, we exercise. When we exercise, our body releases endorphins, the very hormones that block pain. This is why most people feel happy after workouts. However, the happiness is only temporary because the amount of endorphins in our bodies decrease once we stop exercising.
- Once we become successful, we buy everything that we ever wanted—cars, clothes, home. Each time we acquire something, our brains release dopamine which is a 'pleasure' hormone. Dopamine helps motivate us to work hard so that we can experience the pleasure of the reward. However, once the initial wave of achievement subsides, dopamine production in our body also drops.
- The next happiness hormone, oxytocin, is the easiest to get. It is released when we love. For example, when we hug a friend, cuddle with a pet or kiss our spouse, oxytocin is released in varying amounts. Easy, isn't it?
- Serotonin, the last happiness hormone, is released when we do something that benefits others—when we give to causes beyond ourselves and our own benefit. This is why we often see billionaires turning to charity when they have already achieved what they wanted to achieve in life. It is possible that they have had enough dopamine from material pleasures, and they now need the serotonin.

What do happy people do to be happy?

People who are happy seem to intuitively know that their happiness is the sum of their life choices, and that their lives are built on the following pillars that make them content and are responsible for their happiness. These include:

- Devoting time to family and friends
- Appreciating and valuing what they have
- Maintaining an optimistic outlook
- Developing a sense of purpose
- Living in the moment
- Sharing and caring

Did you know that one of the most popular and successful courses at Harvard teaches you how to be happy? The Positive Psychology class attracts 1,400 students per semester and 20 per cent of Harvard graduates take this elective course. The class focuses on happiness, self-esteem and motivation and attempts to gives students the tools necessary to face life with more joy. So, what is it that we can do to make ourselves happier?

- Invest in relationships: Research studies suggest that relationships provide the strongest meaning and purpose to our lives. So cultivate meaningful relationships. Surround yourself with happy people. Give enough time to friends and family who help you celebrate life's successes and support you in difficult times.
- Set realistic goals: Setting goals for ourselves is good. However, goals need to be realistic to avoid disappointment. While we are always being told to aim for the moon, it should be one that we can see clearly, not one that shines over a distant planet.
- Always be nice to people and help those in need: Sharing

happiness multiplies our joy. Simple things like listening to someone's troubles or offering a genuine compliment to someone you appreciate, not only bring smiles to the faces of others, but also contribute to one's own sense of happiness and contentment.

- Have fun: Do something that makes you happy. Meditate, pursue a hobby, find your passion, find something you love doing and work towards it. Take up classes to learn new things.
- Eat sensibly: Eat light meals at regular intervals and keep your glucose levels stable. Avoid excess of anything in your diet. Keep carbohydrates and sugar to a low level.
- Exercise: Sweating it out is rather important in the quest towards contentment. Exercising releases endorphins or happiness hormones that help us keep ourselves in good health and happy.
- Cultivate optimism: Develop the habit of seeing the positive side of life. This does not mean that we need to be overly optimistic— after all, bad things do happen. It would be silly to pretend otherwise. However, we don't have to let the negatives colour our whole outlook on life.
- Live in the moment: The American writer Robert Brault says, 'Enjoy the little things, for one day you may look back and realise they were the big things.' The point is don't postpone celebration or being happy waiting for a day when your life is less busy or less stressful. That day may never come. Instead, look for opportunities to enjoy the small pleasures of everyday life. The

Indian spiritual guru Osho said, 'Enjoy simple things with total intensity. Just a cup of tea can be a deep meditation.'

- Practice relaxation techniques: Meditation, listening to music and yoga are useful ways to bring our emotions into balance. Try and practise them. It is proven that listening to music awakens you to sing, this will make your life happy because of the additional dopamine release.
- Feel attractive: 70 per cent of people say they feel happier when they think they look good. Take care of yourself. To have good emotional health, it's important to take care of your body by eating healthy, getting enough sleep, and exercising regularly. Also, stay away from addictions.
- Laugh: Swap jokes, watch your favourite sitcom or funny YouTube video, actively pursue humour. Don't skip the cartoon strip of your newspaper. Read funny stuff. Spend time with friends who have a sense of humour. There are tremendous mood-boosting effects of laugher, but more on that later.
- Talk: Keeping feelings of sadness inside can make you feel worse. It is fine to let your loved ones know when something is bothering you, even if they might not be able to offer solutions to all your problems. Seek professional help if required.
- Develop resilience: This enables one to cope with stress in a healthy way. Resilience can be learned and strengthened with strategies like having strong

social support, keeping a positive view of yourself, and accepting change. A counsellor, spiritual advisor or therapist can help you achieve this with cognitive behavioural therapy (CBT).
- Positive focus: Focus on the good things in life and try not to obsess about the problems at work, school or home. This leads to negative feelings. This does not however mean you have to pretend to be happy when you feel stressed, anxious or upset. It is important to deal with these negative feelings, but try to focus on the positive things in your life, too. You can write a diary to keep track of things that make you happy. Think of people who make you happy. Having a positive outlook can improve your quality of life and give your health a boost. More on this later.
- Avoid negativity: Avoid associating with those who are always complaining about life. Such people may ruin your positive thought process. Avoid such people. Do not poison peace by anger. Anger defeats the very purpose for which it is aroused. Anger is not an antidote for anger. So try not to get angry and be patient. The Buddha famously said, 'You will not be punished for your anger but by it.'

Power of positive thinking

Do you know that our brains produce as many as 12,000-50,000 thoughts per day? For some people who tend to think a lot, estimates run as high as 60,000 thoughts in a day. Is it bad to have thoughts running in our minds continuously?

Well, nothing wrong with it; what's disturbing, however, is that the vast majority of thoughts are pure nonsense.

There is a wonderful statement variously attributed to Ralph Waldo Emerson, Lao Tzu, Buddha and others. It goes something like this:

Watch your thoughts, they become words.
Watch your words, they become actions.
Watch your actions, they become habits.
Watch your habits, they become your character.
Watch your character, it becomes your destiny.

It all starts with a thought, the most potent form of energy. Mahatma Gandhi said, 'A man is but the product of his thoughts.' Believe it or not, majority of us either dwell in the past, are obsessed about mistakes we might have made, struggle with guilt, or worry about our future. We constantly drift into fantasy, fiction and negativity. Sadly, for some of us, 70-80 per cent of our daily thoughts are negative. A very small number of our thoughts are actually focused on what is truly important for our present. The astronomer Patrick Moore joked, 'At my age I do what Mark Twain did. I get my daily paper, look at the obituaries page and if I'm not there I carry on as usual.'

The power of thought is the power of positive thinking. This does not mean that we spend our life meditating. What it actually means is that unpleasant thoughts can be dealt in a better and more productive way. Consider an example:

The power of positive thinking is what actor and singer Raageshwari Loomba Swaroop strongly believes in. It has been a journey of huge highs and lows for Raageshwari after she was diagnosed with Bell's Palsy—a disorder in which the muscles in your face paralyse temporarily. Says Raageshwari, 'It was quite bizarre to wake up one morning and feel that my left face was completely numb and powerless. Steroids were given to me right away but they played havoc with my system. I discontinued them soon, as I could see my mental and physical make-up was changing dramatically. Intense weight gain, lethargy, mood swings and new illnesses simply started an unstoppable chain reaction. I had to truly find my own strength deep down. Trust me it's actually always between just you and your mind.' It was the positivity of thoughts that kept her going. Today, Raageshwari has recovered from her medical condition and advocates the benefits of positive thinking. She says, 'The key in living life is being positive. They say you cannot contain two thoughts in your mind at the same time. So, let's choose the positive thought and keep at it.'

All thoughts whether positive or negative start with self-talk. Self-talk is an endless process of unspoken thoughts, which keep running in our head. Most people do not realise it, but as we go about our daily lives, we are constantly thinking about and interpreting the situations we find ourselves in. It is like having an internal voice inside our head that determines how we perceive every situation. Psychologists call this inner voice 'self-talk', and it includes our conscious thoughts as well as our unconscious assumptions or beliefs.

Something like 'I'm sure I'm going to fail at this' or 'I'm in a hopeless situation. I feel like giving up' are examples of negative self-talk. Whereas something like 'If I prepare well for my exam, I am sure I will do well', or 'I am really looking forward to that match. I hope to win it' are positive self-talks.

An unnamed wise man correctly wrote, 'Dear optimist, pessimist, and realist, while you guys were arguing about the glass of water, I drank it. Sincerely, the opportunist.' Drink!

Life purpose

The great poet Omar Khayyam in his *Rubaiyat* said, 'Ah make the most of what yet we may spend, before we too into dust descend!' While one can't be certain of the angle from which Khayyam was approaching the subject, one can be certain that have a fulfilling life makes sense.

Benjamin Mays, the civil rights leader, wryly commented, 'The tragedy of life doesn't lie in not reaching your goal. The tragedy lies in having no goal to reach.' And that's at the heart of the matter.

The present-day concept of 'life purpose' is derived from the papers of Viktor Frankl, a Jewish physician trained in psychiatry and neurology. He survived three terrible years in Nazi concentration camps, including Auschwitz. Frankl came to the conclusion that having a purpose in life helped him survive. We need for our lives to have some meaning. It's a fundamental human need almost as important as exercise and nutritious diet.

Frankl formulated a set of thirteen questions as a means of measuring purpose. A couple of decades later, researchers Crumbaugh and Maholick developed his work further with a 20-question list that is even today used and has been found quite effective in quantifying life purpose.

There is associative evidence that purpose can help solve problems such as addiction, depression and anxiety. Recently, researchers are finding that purpose can possibly protect even against Alzheimer's. Yet more studies correlate purpose with reduced possibilities of stroke, heart attack and general mortality. The French biologist Jean Rostand correctly observed that a man is not old as long as he is seeking something. Holding on to the belief that your life has a purpose seems to provide you with a resilience—almost like a barrier against stress.

The great heavyweight boxer Muhammad Ali said, 'Don't count the days, make the days count.' And the great American President, Abraham Lincoln, said, 'In the end it's not the years in your life that count, it's the life in your years.' What are all these statements trying to tell us? Simply that a purpose in life can make your life better, and contentment and happiness play a vital role in our health.

Key Takeaways

- There is no true health without happiness. If happiness is the house you want to build, contentment is the foundation for constructing that house.

- We often fail to understand that our physical and emotional health are interrelated. It's time we realise that seeking medical help for emotional problems is not a sign of weakness.

- Emotionally healthy people are those who can control their emotions and do not allow those emotions to play on their minds and bodies.
- There are four chemicals related to happiness—endorphins, dopamine, oxytocin and serotonin. The more we can produce, the happier we are.
- What can we do to be happier? Invest in relationships, set realistic goals for yourself, be nice to people, have fun, eat sensibly, exercise, cultivate optimism, live in the moment, practice relaxation techniques, feel attractive, laugh, talk, develop resilience, focus on positives and avoid negativity.
- Positive thinking does not mean that we spend our life meditating. What it actually means is that unpleasant thoughts can be dealt in a better and more productive way.
- Holding on to the belief that your life has a purpose seems to provide you with a resilience—almost like a barrier against stress.

STEP FOURTEEN: PERSONALISE

So you thought we only have thirteen little steps to help you become healthier. Well, here's the little surprise. We actually have fourteen steps—one extra step, because, what effort is complete without going the extra mile? What is that extra step without which all these prior steps have absolutely no meaning? In one word—personalise.

To broadly summarise, the steps to good health are almost common sense:

1. Sleep: Sleep is more important than food or water. Poor sleep can be caused by a multitude of factors including pain, stress, acidity, irritable bowels, depression, environment, etc. Getting adequate quantity and quality of both REM and NREM sleep is vital. During the sleep cycle your body undergoes maintenance, growth hormones are released and wounds are healed. It also helps in processing memories and building new skills. Lack of sleep can cause poor immunity, obesity, depression and even substance abuse. Good sleep can enhance athletic performance, memory,

decision-making and brain function. You can sleep better by blocking out noise and light, taking melatonin supplements, following a routine, exercising regularly, managing room temperature, avoiding heavy meals and alcohol or stimulants before bedtime, limiting fluid intake and sleeping on a comfortable mattress and pillows.

2. Hydrate: Your body should be a reflection of earth. Adult bodies should be at least 70 per cent water. If you experience a dry mouth, thirst, headaches, dizziness, drowsiness or constipation then these are possible signs of dehydration. Water helps your body detox, ensures that your kidneys function properly, cleans your gut, promotes weight loss, reduces water retention, regulates blood pressure and cholesterol, lubricates your joints, reduces allergies and headaches, reduces instances of kidney stones, improves mood, slows ageing, improves mental performance, and improves skin condition and complexion. You should aim to drink two to three litres of water per day. Quality of water is as important as quantity. Use filtered and boiled water instead of RO water.

3. Nourish: Food is medicine and vital in ensuring good health. Follow a balanced diet rather than a crash diet. A balanced diet is one that gives your body all the nutrients it needs to function correctly. The answer to good nutrition lies in two words: sense and moderation. Your daily diet can include items from the five major

groups—grains, vegetables and legumes, fruit, dairy and lean meats. How you eat is as important as what you eat. Eat slowly. Eat your last meal at least three hours before turning in. Try to get maximum nutrition from unprocessed foods, preferably organic. Cooking at home is better than eating out. Maintain an acid-alkaline balance. Use a natural probiotic.

4. Move: The human body actually craves exercise; humans having originally been hunter-gatherers. The benefits of exercise include mood improvement, better sleep, weight loss, cardio health, regulated blood sugar, higher fertility and libido, better posture and flexibility, better bone density and muscle tone, reduced asthma, reduced blood pressure and belly fat, reduced arthritic pain, improved brain health and memory, higher energy levels and improved skin. There are four key types of exercise—cardio, strength, flexibility and unsitting. Sitting is the new smoking. Avoid long stretches of sitting, even at work. Aim for at least thirty minutes of physical activity five times a week. Use a step monitor and aim for 10,000 steps per day.

5. Digest: For good health, we only need 80 per cent of our gut bacteria to be good. The remaining 20 per cent can be bad. Wrong balance of gut bacteria can cause many problems including inflammatory or irritable bowel, Crohn's disease, obesity, type-2 diabetes, heart disease, anxiety, depression, colon cancer, arthritis, low immunity and leaky gut. You can do many things to

improve the bacterial balance of your gut. These include eating more fibre, avoiding antibiotics, ensuring timely bowel movements, exercising, avoiding processed foods, reducing gluten intake, using probiotics and prebiotics, adding fermented foods to your diet, eating slowly, getting adequate sleep, meditating and curing leaky gut.

6. Alkalise: Mildly acidic compounds are needed within our bodies to keep tissues firm and supple. Alkalinity is needed for fluidity, flexibility and relaxation in the body. Ideally, we need a balance between acidity and alkalinity. There are many possible reasons for acid build-up. These include alcohol dependence, drug use, overuse of antibiotics, poor digestion or gut health, low fibre consumption, excessive meat consumption, etc. Balanced pH has several benefits for the human body. These include reduced internal inflammation, greater protection from heart disease, lower diabetes risk and stronger bone density. There are several things you can do to achieve a balanced pH. These include lowering your intake of acidic foods, consuming an alkaline diet, drinking alkaline water, lowering your medicine intake, managing stress and better digestion.

7. Breathe: Every human takes around 20,000 breaths per day. As babies we breathe deeply but our breathing pattern changes as we age. Tension and stress force us to breathe in a shallower manner that is not good for us. Setting aside some time in the day for deep breathing into the abdomen is a healthy practice. Plan your deep

breathing during the day in the way that you would schedule business appointments in your diary. Two ten-minute slots each day are ideal. There are some simple pranayama exercises such as bhastrika, kapalbhati, brhamari, anulom vilom and bahya pranayam that can help you improve your health through breath. There are many benefits of deep breathing. These benefits include calming the mind, relaxing the muscles, cleaning the lungs, lowered heart rate, releasing toxins, lowering blood pressure, improving sleep, strengthening immunity, improving digestion and enhancing memory.

8. Supplement: The golden rule is to get your nutrients from whole foods first and then supplement only if needed. Assuming that you eat a well-balanced diet and lead a healthy life, there is still a strong case for supplements that can take care of specific deficiencies that you may be experiencing at that given point in time. Taking supplements should not become a free-for-all. Some supplements have side effects and it is best to take advice of a doctor before taking them. Some of the supplements that you may consider: fish oil, probiotics, vitamin D, magnesium, brahmi, protein, calcium, ajwain, ashwagandha, haldi, zinc, elaichi, jeera, mulaithi, manjistha, neem, iron, vitamin C, dalchini, spirulina, glucosamine, tulsi and sesamin.

9. Love: Love must start with self-love, which is the art of self-acceptance. It means having self-respect and a positive self-image. Loving yourself also means investing

in your own health. You can do several things to love yourself—remind yourself that you are important, stop blaming yourself for things that go wrong, do one thing each day that makes you happy, think positive and create a support system. Any two people who love, support, encourage and help each other practically as well as emotionally can share a positive relationship that makes it easier to handle the stresses and pressures of life. Beneficial romantic relationships can lower stress, improve your body's healing power, add years to your life, encourage healthier habits and promote healthy intimacy. It has been shown that keeping a pet can have significant health benefits, too. Some of the things that you can do to maintain a healthy relationship are honest and open communication, empathy, acceptance, being a good listener, showing appreciation, providing emotional support, laughing together and keeping the playfulness alive.

10. Prevent: Pay attention to your body. It sends signals if something needs to be fixed within. Remember, a stitch in time saves nine. In particular, your hair, skin, oral health, weight, urine colour, snoring, fatigue and stools, they all have hidden indicators of potential illnesses. Get medical check-ups at regular frequency according to your age and gender. Some of the key markers to consider in these check-ups are cholesterol, diabetes, blood pressure, body mass index (BMI), breast and cervical health, colorectal cancer screening, oral health,

immunisation schedules, prostate health, viral hepatitis, HIV/AIDS screening and blood tests to evaluate body organs like liver, kidneys, heart and thyroid.

11. Moderate: Addiction is usually triggered by you being hungry, angry, lonely or tired. Drug addiction can include stimulants, depressants, hallucinogens, dissociatives, opioids, inhalants and cannabis. There is nothing like moderation when it comes to drugs. Every user will eventually get addicted and so it's best to stay away. Digital addiction is affecting children and adults. Create no-technology hours and zones to avoid addiction. Work addiction is real. It is the 'high' achieved from extra work. It eventually can take a toll on your health and family life. Nicotine is one of the most addictive substances known to man. There are many possibilities these days to quit the habit with the support of nicotine patches, gum, inhalers and sprays. Relationship, sexual and porn addiction also call for counselling or lifestyle changes. Rehabilitation from alcohol addiction requires a lifetime commitment and involves lifestyle changes along with group support such as Alcoholics Anonymous (AA). The key lies in moderation—be it food, alcohol, exercise, caffeine, sleep or digital.

12. Relax: Stress results in a rush of hormones such as cortisol into your bloodstream. This leads to increased heart rate, tensed muscles and quicker and shallower breathing. While we can't avoid the triggers that cause stress in our lives, we can determine far better ways

of reacting to them. One of the ways is the relaxation response—this includes breath focus, body scan, mindfulness meditation, guided imagery, chanting, yoga or tai chi. Other methods include massage therapy, laughter therapy, hydrotherapy, aromatherapy, music and art therapy, and biofeedback.

13. Rejoice: There is no true health without happiness. If happiness is the house you want to build, contentment is the foundation for constructing that house. We often fail to understand that our physical and emotional health are interrelated. It's time we realise that seeking medical help for emotional problems is not a sign of weakness. Emotionally healthy people are those who can control their emotions and do not allow those emotions to play on their minds and bodies. There are four chemicals related to happiness—endorphins, dopamine, oxytocin and serotonin. The more we can produce, the happier we are. What can we do to be happier? Invest in relationships, set realistic goals for yourself, be nice to people, have fun, eat sensibly, exercise, cultivate optimism, live in the moment, practice relaxation techniques, feel attractive, laugh, talk, develop resilience, focus on positives and avoid negativity. Positive thinking does not mean that we spend our life meditating. What it actually means is that unpleasant thoughts can be dealt in a better and more productive way. Holding on to the belief that your life has a purpose provides you with a resilience—almost like a barrier against stress.

We have presented hundreds of facts in this little book—tips for healthy eating, lifestyle, clean gut, exercise, alkalinity, moderation, breathing and the like. We have thrown lots of advice your way. Probably this may not be the first health book that you have perused. In addition, a simple visit to Google-baba would have thrown up millions of websites, each purporting to have the ideal mantras for good health. The point that I wish to make is this: one size does not fit all. It's usually different strokes for different folks.

You need to pick and choose what works for *you*. For example, some individuals are happiest with intense exercise whereas others are satisfied to simply walk or bike a few times in the week. There are those for whom happiness lies in friendships and socialising while others find contentment in charitable work or working towards a business or creative goal. One particular individual may find that a ketogenic diet helps her lose weight while another may find that a calorie-restricted diet works better. If you truly want to get results from this book, look at it as a broad guideline and use the options listed to find what works for you. But within each of these steps there lies a world of possibilities. The trick lies in adapting all the various options into a list of tasks that you believe will work for you.

A sandwich is two slices of bread containing a filling in the middle but one sandwich is remarkably different from another. Think Bombay Sandwich versus Bacon-Lettuce-Tomato versus Peanut Butter and Jelly versus Grilled Cheese. Truly different tastes, textures and nutritional values. Your health programme is your own personalised sandwich. Type it up or handwrite it on a sheet of paper so that it becomes a reminder of what you wish to do to achieve better health.

The ancient Greek tragedian, Aeschylus, observed, 'There's nothing certain in a man's life except this—that he must lose it.' True. All of us are going to die someday. But as William Wallace said, 'Every man dies. Not every man really lives.' That's precisely the point of this book—how one can live better.

We have thrown so much information at you, it can get a little overwhelming. There are two ladies who would like to help you remember the content better. They are Mrs Bland and Mrs HP. Just remember the letters of 'Mrs Bland Mrs HP' as a mnemonic.

M—Move
R—Relax
S—Sleep

B—Breathe
L—Love
A—Alkalise
N—Nourish
D—Digest

M—Moderate
R—Rejoice
S—Supplement

H—Hydrate
P—Prevent

REFERENCES

1. 10 Reasons Why Good Sleep Is Important, Joe Leech, https://www.healthline.com/nutrition/10-reasons-why-good-sleep-is-important
2. 45 Alarming Statistics on Americans' Caffeine Consumption, https://www.thediabetescouncil.com/45-alarming-statistics-on-americans-caffeine-consumption/
3. 5 areas sleep has the greatest impact on athletic performance, *Fatigue Science*, https://www.fatiguescience.com/blog/5-ways-sleep-impacts-peak-athletic-performance/
4. 50% of Indian teenagers prone to mobile phone addiction, https://telecom.economictimes.indiatimes.com/news/50-of-indian-teenagers-prone-to-mobile-phone-addiction/51069205
5. A randomized controlled trial of the effect of aerobic exercise training on feelings of energy and fatigue in sedentary young adults with persistent fatigue, Puetz, Flowers, O'Connor, https://www.ncbi.nlm.nih.gov/pubmed/18277063
6. American Academy of Pediatrics Announces New Recommendations for Children's Media Use, https://www.aap.org/en-us/about-the-aap/aap-press-room/Pages/American-Academy-of-Pediatrics-Announces-New-Recommendations-for-Childrens-Media-Use.aspx
7. Are You Addicted to Your Smartphone, The California State University, https://www2.calstate.edu/csu-system/news/Pages/are-you-addicted-to-your-smartphone.aspx
8. Australian Guide to Healthy Eating, http://www.foodstandards.gov.au/science/monitoringnutrients/australianhealthsurveyandaustraliandietaryguidelines/classification/Pages/default.aspx
9. Bacteria in the gut may lead to anxiety, depression, https://economictimes.indiatimes.com/magazines/panache/bacteria-in-the-gut-may-lead-to-anxiety-depression/articleshow/64634726.cms
10. Be smart with your smartphones, PatientMD, https://patientmd.com/blog/be-smart-with-your-smartphones/

11. Caffeine and Kids: FDA Takes a Closer Look, US FDA, https://www.fda.gov/ForConsumers/ConsumerUpdates/ucm350570.htm
12. Changing gut bacteria through diet affects brain function UCLA study shows, http://newsroom.ucla.edu/releases/changing-gut-bacteria-through-245617
13. Crime in India 2013, National Crime Record Bureau, https://www.firstpost.com/living/lakh-suicides-take-place-india-every-year-report-1601231.html
14. Distracted Driving in India-A study on Mobile Phone Usage, Pattern & Behaviour, Save Life Foundation, http://savelifefoundation.org/wp-content/uploads/2017/04/Distracted-Driving-in-India_A-Study-on-Mobile-Phone-Usage-Pattern-and-Behaviour.pdf
15. Distracted Eating May Add to Weight Gain, Howard LeWine, Harvard Health Publishing, https://www.health.harvard.edu/blog/distracted-eating-may-add-to-weight-gain-201303296037
16. Dreams: Why do we dream? Hannah Nichols, https://www.medicalnewstoday.com/articles/284378.php
17. Driver Fatigue and Road Safety - Implication in an Indian Context, Rahul Dagli, https://www.researchgate.net/publication/307598070_DRIVER_FATIGUE_AND_ROAD_SAFETY_-IMPLICATION_IN_AN_INDIAN_CONTEXT
18. Durability of Effect of Massage Therapy on Blood Pressure, Mahshid Givi, https://www.ncbi.nlm.nih.gov/pmc/articles/PMC3733180/
19. Effect of controlled deep breathing on psychomotor and higher mental functions in normal individuals, https://www.ncbi.nlm.nih.gov/pubmed/26571983
20. Effect of exercise type on smoking cessation: a meta-analysis of randomized controlled trials, https://www.ncbi.nlm.nih.gov/pmc/articles/PMC5585974/
21. Effect of Left, Right and Alternate Nostril Breathing on Verbal and Spatial Memory, https://www.ncbi.nlm.nih.gov/pmc/articles/PMC4800515/
22. Effect of Regular Yogic Training on Growth Hormone and

Dehydroepiandrosterone Sulfate as an Endocrine Marker of Aging, https://www.ncbi.nlm.nih.gov/pmc/articles/PMC4034508/
23. Effect of Slow Breathing Training For a Month on Blood Pressure and Heart Rate Variability in Healthy Subjects, Swarnalatha Nagarajan, https://www.ejmanager.com/mnstemps/28/28-1398946807.pdf
24. Effects of changes in water intake on mood of high and low drinkers, https://www.ncbi.nlm.nih.gov/pubmed/24728141
25. *Every Man's Guide to Homeopathy* by Mukesh Batra, Asia Book Corp
26. *Food Rules: An Eater's Manual*, Michael Pollan, Penguin
27. Global Depression Statistics, World Health Organization World Mental Health Survey Initiative, https://www.independent.co.uk/life-style/health-and-families/health-news/india-named-worlds-most-depressed-nation-2325927.html
28. Happy Marriage, Healthy Heart, Alexandra Sifferlin, Time, http://healthland.time.com/2012/03/07/happy-marriage-happy-heart/
29. *Healing with Homeopathy* by Mukesh Batra, Jaico Publishing
30. Health Risks from Drinking Demineralized Water, Frantisek Kozisek, National Institute of Public Health, http://www.who.int/water_sanitation_health/dwq/nutrientschap12.pdf
31. Here's How Many Days A Person Can Survive Without Water, Dina Spector, https://www.businessinsider.in/Heres-How-Many-Days-A-Person-Can-Survive-Without-Water/articleshow/34889866.cms
32. How much screen time is healthy for children, Simon Jary, https://www.techadvisor.co.uk/feature/digital-home/how-much-screen-time-for-kids-3520917/
33. How Much Sleep Do Babies and Kids Need? https://www.sleepfoundation.org/excessivesleepiness/content/how-much-sleep-do-babies-and-kids-need
34. *How Not To Die: Discover the foods scientifically proven to prevent and reverse disease*, Michael Greger, Pan Books
35. How to Hydrate Properly, https://lapetitecheff.wordpress.com/2018/06/01/how-to-hydrate-properly-cum-sa-te-hidratezi-corect/

36. Instagram ranked worst for young people's mental health, Royal Society for Public Health, https://www.rsph.org.uk/about-us/news/instagram-ranked-worst-for-young-people-s-mental-health.html
37. Late-breaking study finds aerobic exercise significantly improved asthma control, American College of Chest Physicians, http://www.chestnet.org/News/Press-Releases/2015/10/Late-breaking-study-finds-aerobic-exercise-significantly-improved-asthma-control
38. Laughing Can Help You Lose Weight, Helen Pilcher, https://www.telegraph.co.uk/news/health/news/4221778/Laughing-can-help-you-lose-weight.html
39. Laughter Can Keep The Weight Off, *International Journal of Obesity*, http://news.bbc.co.uk/2/hi/health/6274119.stm
40. Loneliness Is As Bad For Your Health As Smoking 15 Cigarettes A Day, https://www.iflscience.com/health-and-medicine/loneliness-is-as-bad-for-your-health-as-smoking-15-cigarettes-a-day/
41. Love & Pain Relief, Tara Parker-Pope, *New York Times*, https://well.blogs.nytimes.com/2010/10/13/love-and-pain-relief/
42. Managing Irritable Bowel Syndrome-How to help patients control this life-altering condition, Anastasi and Capili, https://www.ncbi.nlm.nih.gov/pmc/articles/PMC5654469/
43. Moderate Sleep Deprivation Produces Impairments in Cognitive and Motor Performance Equivalent to Legally Prescribed Levels of Alcohol Intoxication, A Williamson and A. Feyer, https://www.ncbi.nlm.nih.gov/pmc/articles/PMC1739867/pdf/v057p00649.pdf
44. Overworked interns prone to medical errors, William J. Cromie, https://news.harvard.edu/gazette/story/2004/10/overworked-interns-prone-to-medical-errors/
45. Q: What do songbirds dream about? A: Singing, Michael McCarthy, https://www.independent.co.uk/environment/q-what-do-songbirds-dream-about-a-singing-634062.html
46. Relaxation technique and postoperative pain in patients undergoing

cardiac surgery, Miller and Perry, https://www.ncbi.nlm.nih.gov/pubmed/2180861
47. Sexual frequency and salivary immunoglobulin A (IgA), https://www.ncbi.nlm.nih.gov/pubmed/15217036
48. Sleep and Depression, Tsuno, Besset and Ritchie, US National Library of Medicine, https://www.ncbi.nlm.nih.gov/pubmed/16259539
49. Some of My Best Friends Are Germs, Michael Pollanmay, *New York Times*, https://www.nytimes.com/2013/05/19/magazine/say-hello-to-the-100-trillion-bacteria-that-make-up-your-microbiome.html
50. Study: Physical Activity Impacts Overall Quality of Sleep, National Sleep Foundation, https://www.sleepfoundation.org/sleep-news/study-physical-activity-impacts-overall-quality-sleep
51. Sudarshan Kriya Yogic Breathing in the Treatment of Stress, Anxiety, and Depression: Part II-Clinical Applications and Guidelines, Brown, Gerbarg, *The Journal of Alternative and Complementary Medicine*, https://www.liebertpub.com/doi/abs/10.1089/acm.2005.11.711
52. *The Blood Sugar Solution*, Mark Hyman, Little Brown & Co.
53. The Effect of Diaphragmatic Breathing on Attention, Negative Affect and Stress in Healthy Adults, https://www.ncbi.nlm.nih.gov/pmc/articles/PMC5455070/
54. The Effect of Humor on Short-term Memory in Older Adults: a New Component for Whole-person Wellness, US National Library of Medicine, https://www.ncbi.nlm.nih.gov/pubmed/24682001
55. The effects of sleep extension on the athletic performance of collegiate basketball players, Mah, Kezirian and Dement, US National Library of Medicine, https://www.ncbi.nlm.nih.gov/pubmed/21731144
56. *The Happiness Trap*, Russ Harris, Trumpeter
57. The Problem With Drowsy Driving, National Sleep Foundation, https://www.sleepfoundation.org/sleep-news/the-problem-drowsy-driving

58. The Spread of Sleep Loss Influences Drug Use in Adolescent Social Networks, Mednick, Christakis and Fowler, US National Library of Medicine, https://www.ncbi.nlm.nih.gov/pmc/articles/PMC2841645/
59. *The Wellness Sense: A Practical Guide to your Physical and Emotional Health Based on Ayurvedic and Yogic Wisom*, Om Swami, Element India
60. Water, Hydration & Health, Popkin, D'Anci and Rosenberg, https://www.ncbi.nlm.nih.gov/pmc/articles/PMC2908954/
61. What is Good Quality Sleep, National Sleep Foundation, https://www.sleepfoundation.org/press-release/what-good-quality-sleep
62. What Your Gut Bacteria Say About You, WebMD, https://www.webmd.com/digestive-disorders/what-your-gut-bacteria-say-your-health#1
63. World Sleep Day: 93% Indians are sleep-deprived, Jayanta Deka, https://timesofindia.indiatimes.com/city/lucknow/World-Sleep-Day-93-Indians-are-sleep-deprived/articleshow/46547288.cms
64. Yogic breathing when compared to attention control reduces the levels of pro-inflammatory biomarkers in saliva: a pilot randomized controlled trial, https://www.ncbi.nlm.nih.gov/pubmed/27538513
65. Your gut is the cornerstone of your immune system, Health24, https://www.health24.com/Medical/Flu/Preventing-flu/your-gut-is-the-cornerstone-of-your-immune-system-20160318

www.ingramcontent.com/pod-product-compliance
Lightning Source LLC
La Vergne TN
LVHW021221080526
838199LV00089B/5625